D1827187

Belinda Smith

Engaging Adult Learners using E-Learning Technologies

Belinda Smith

Engaging Adult Learners using E-Learning Technologies

Scholar's Press

Impressum / Imprint

Bibliografische Information der Deutschen Nationalbibliothek: Die Deutsche Nationalbibliothek verzeichnet diese Publikation in der Deutschen Nationalbibliografie; detaillierte bibliografische Daten sind im Internet über http://dnb.d-nb.de abrufbar.
Alle in diesem Buch genannten Marken und Produktnamen unterliegen warenzeichen-, marken- oder patentrechtlichem Schutz bzw. sind Warenzeichen oder eingetragene Warenzeichen der jeweiligen Inhaber. Die Wiedergabe von Marken, Produktnamen, Gebrauchsnamen, Handelsnamen, Warenbezeichnungen u.s.w. in diesem Werk berechtigt auch ohne besondere Kennzeichnung nicht zu der Annahme, dass solche Namen im Sinne der Warenzeichen- und Markenschutzgesetzgebung als frei zu betrachten wären und daher von jedermann benutzt werden dürften.

Bibliographic information published by the Deutsche Nationalbibliothek: The Deutsche Nationalbibliothek lists this publication in the Deutsche Nationalbibliografie; detailed bibliographic data are available in the Internet at http://dnb.d-nb.de.
Any brand names and product names mentioned in this book are subject to trademark, brand or patent protection and are trademarks or registered trademarks of their respective holders. The use of brand names, product names, common names, trade names, product descriptions etc. even without a particular marking in this work is in no way to be construed to mean that such names may be regarded as unrestricted in respect of trademark and brand protection legislation and could thus be used by anyone.

Coverbild / Cover image: www.ingimage.com

Verlag / Publisher:
Scholar's Press
ist ein Imprint der / is a trademark of
OmniScriptum GmbH & Co. KG
Heinrich-Böcking-Str. 6-8, 66121 Saarbrücken, Deutschland / Germany
Email: info@scholars-press.com

Herstellung: siehe letzte Seite /
Printed at: see last page
ISBN: 978-3-639-76407-9

Zugl. / Approved by: Minneapolis, Capella University, Diss., 2010

Abstract

The convergence of competition, cost, technology, and new consumer demands have suggested that there are different rules for engaging students in a historically placid environment that has derived its strength from tradition rather than transition (Beaudoin, 2002, Distance education leadership: An essential role for the new century). The adult learner population is growing both in number and in proportion to the traditional student population (National Center for Educational Statistics, 2007, Digest of education statistics: 2007). Adult learners enroll in online distance education courses hoping they will be able to fit acquiring a degree into their busy lives (Kasworm, 2003, Setting the stage: Adults in higher education). However, between 40% to 80% drop out of online classes (Tyler-Smith, 2006, Early attrition among first time elearners: A review of factors that contribute to drop-out, withdrawal and non-completion rates of adult learners undertaking elearning programmes) and 21% are pleading for a more engaging online experience (Schaffhauser, 2009, Survey reports many online learners never seek help before dropping out). Confusion increases as higher education leaders explore dozens of new e-learning technologies to engage learners (Kim & Bonk, 2006, The future of online teaching and learning in higher education: The survey says). The purpose of this quantitative study is to compare two types of adult learners – adult learners enrolled on an online campus and adult learners enrolled on blended campuses – and their selection of e-learning technologies to engage their instructor, course content, and other learners in a virtual classroom. In a learner-centered world, student selection of e-learning technologies may better predict how to engage students in an online distance education course (Kim & Bonk, 2006; Percival & Muirhead, 2009, Prioritizing the implementation of e-learning tools to enhance the post-secondary learning environment).

Dedications

I dedicate this dissertation to my grandmother, Jessie Lee Wilson. I love you "Mamo" just as much as when you were in this world physically. Your spiritual presence and my memories of our talks, handholding, and smiles taught me that showing unconditional love is how to become great. Yes, "Mamo" you are right. Those who serve others gladly become great unknowingly. They also live forever in stories told about the love they demonstrated.

Secondly, I would like to dedicate this dissertation to Bishop J. H. Sherman. Although you are not here with me physically, your inspiration and belief in me during my youth is the reason for this dissertation journey. Your prophecy was correct. Thank you for believing in me. Thank you for teaching me and allowing me to teach in my youth. Thank you for allowing me to perform duties that have led me to this station in life. I dedicate this dissertation to you, too.

"Mamo" and Bishop, thank you for instilling in me at a young age that faith without works or works without faith will not accomplish anything. Also, thank you for showing me that it is not how much you give or what you give, but why you give. God knows our hearts and sees our actions. Thank you both for allowing me to sit at your feet and relish in your knowledge. I love you both.

Acknowledgement

First, I would like to acknowledge my great-great grandmother who raised my grandmother. Thank you for rearing my inspiration. I would like to acknowledge my husband, Raymond E. Smith, Jr. I would not have been able to pursue a doctoral degree or complete this dissertation without my husband's support. I would like to acknowledge my mother, Quilla Lendon, for her encouragement. I would like to acknowledge my father, Lucius Lendon, for coming home from work to help me understand my homework when I was a child. I would like to acknowledge my children, Carlton Smith and Cora Outling, and my son-in-law, Justin Outling, for believing that I can achieve anything I set my mind to. I would like to acknowledge my grandchildren, Kimbreuna and Kolton Smith, for being my motivation.

I would like to acknowledge Dr. Jennifer Percival and Dr. Bill Muirhead for allowing me to use their survey in this study. I would like to acknowledge my dissertation committee Dr. McLaughlin, Dr. Wishart, and Dr. McNaughton for assisting me with my dissertation. I would like to acknowledge Dr. Tavakoli for being a positive force during my pursuit of my graduate and post graduate degrees. I would like to thank my sponsor and the administrators of the university used in this study. Thank you for being a part of my journey. Live with peace, love, and happiness.

Table of Contents

Acknowledgments.. iv

List of Tables viii

List of Figures ix

CHAPTER 1. INTRODUCTION 1

Introduction to the Problem 1

Background of Study 2

Statement of the Problem.. 6

Purpose of the Study 7

Rationale 7

Research Questions.. 7

Significance of the Study 9

Definition of Terms... 9

Assumption and Limitations 16

Theoretical Framework 16

Summary 17

Organization of the Remainder of the Study 18

CHAPTER 2. LITERATURE REVIEW 19

Overview 19

Introduction to the Internet 20

Facilitating Learning 20

The Adult Learner.. 25

Online Distance Education... 28

Online and Blended Campuses 31

Learners' Internet Usage.. 34

Summary 43

CHAPTER 3. METHODOLOGY 45

Research Design.. 45

Sample... 47

Setting 48

Instrument / Measures.. 51

Data Collection 52

Data Analysis 53

Validity and Reliability.. 54

Ethical Considerations 56

CHAPTER 4. RESULTS 57

Introduction.. 57

Analysis... 58

Examination of Hypotheses 60

Summary 73

CHAPTER 5. DISCUSSION, IMPLICATIONS, RECOMMENDATIONS 74

Introduction.. 74

Discussion 74

Implication for Future Research 79

Recommendations... 81

Conclusion 83

Summary 87

REFERENCES.. 89

APPENDIX A. ADULT LEARNERS' DEMOGRAPHICS 95

APPENDIX B. E-LEARNING MEDIA USE BY AGE CHI-SQUARE GOODNESS 97

APPENDIX C. E-LEARNING MEDIA USE BY AGE CHI-SQUARE TEST 102

List of Tables

Table 1. Instrument Liability Statistics 54

Table 2. E-Learning Devices used to Access Instructor, Course Content, or Other Learners 62

Table 3. E-Learning Media used to Access Instructor 64

Table 4. E-Learning Media used to Access Other Learners 65

Table 5. E-Learning Media used to Access Course Content 66

Table 6. Comparative E-Learning Device Use by Campus Type 68

Table 7. Comparative E-Learning Media to Access Instructor 69

Table 8. Comparative E-Learning Media to Access Other Learners 70

Table 9. Comparative E-Learning Media to Access Course Content 72

Table B1. E-Learning Media Use for Adult Learners over 25 97

Table B2. E-Learning Media Use for Adult Learners 25 - 30 98

Table B3. E-Learning Media Use for Adult Learners 30 - 40 99

Table B4. E-Learning Media Use for Adult Learners 40 - 50 100

Table B5. E-Learning Media Use for Adult Learners over 50 101

Table C1. E-Learning Media Use Comparison by Age 102

Table C2. E-Learning Media Use Comparison by Age without Text Messaging 103

List of Figures

Figure 1. Two types of campuses – online and blended 28

Figure A1. Percentage of adult learners by age 86

Figure A2. Percentage of adult learners by occupational status 86

Figure A3. Percentage of adult learners by gender 86

Figure A4. Percentage of adult learners by income 87

Figure A5. Percentage of adult learners by campus type 87

CHAPTER 1. INTRODUCTION

Introduction to the Problem

The adult learner population is growing both in number and in proportion to the traditional student population (McNair, 1998; National Center for Educational Statistics, 2007). Adult learners are self-directed learners that can learn outside traditional classrooms (Knowles, Holton, & Swanson, 2005). Adult learners are seeking educational programs that will allow them to fit acquiring an education into their busy lives (Compton, Cox, & Laanan, 2006). For this reason, online distance education courses have been implemented on campuses across the country (Charlson, 2006). As a result, adult learners are enrolling on campuses that offer online distance education courses (Compton, et al, 2006). However, administrators are confronted with between 40% to 80% of online students dropping out of online classes (Tyler-Smith, 2006) while at least 21% of those dropping out are pleading for richer and more engaging online learning experiences (Kim & Bonk, 2006; Schaffhauser, 2009).

There are several forms of online distance education courses (Ally, 2008). They range from several blended forms to courses provided completely online. During blended and online courses, learners use synchronous and asynchronous online instructional activities to engage their instructor, course content, and other learners (Carter, 2008; Hwong, 2003; Su, 2006; Zhang, 2003). Since a variety of synchronous and asynchronous online instructional activities can be employed to

1

engage the learner (Zhang, 2003), campus leaders are struggling with deciding which synchronous and asynchronous online instructional activities will allow them to complete their mission while engaging learners (Beaudoin, 2002).

The convergence of competition, cost, technology, and new consumer demands have suggested that there are different rules for engaging students in a historically placid environment that has derived its strength from tradition rather than transition (Beaudoin, 2002). Therefore, it seems appropriate to investigate synchronous and asynchronous online instructional activities adult learners use to engage their instructor, course content, and other learners (Adams, 2006; Harriman, 2004). In a learner-centered world, learners' selection of online instructional activities may better predict where campus leaders' future Internet technology investments should be focused (Kim & Bonk, 2006; Percival & Muirhead, 2009).

Background of Study

Distance education is a formal educational process in which the instructions in the course occur when students and instructors are not in the same place (Shale & Gomes, 1998; Southern Association of Colleges and Schools, 2006; National Center for Educational Statistics, 2007). Online distance education is when the learner is at a distance from their instructor and employ some form of e-learning tools to access e-learning media to engage their instructor, course content, and other learners (Ally, 2008). Blended learning has evolved from simply linking traditional classroom training to online distance education to encompassing multiple delivery media that are designed to complement each other and promote learning (Singh, 2003).

Distance education has been employed by colleges since the 1800s (Scott, 2005). As technology changed, colleges implemented these new technologies into their distance education degree programs (Adams, 2006). For example, the train made it easier to deliver correspondence courses to students located away from the traditional campus. As technologies changed, radio, television, audio tapes, and video tapes were employed in distance education (Moore & Kearsley, 2005). In addition, teleconferencing and video-conferencing via satellite communication have been employed in distance education courses (Moore & Kearsley, 2005; Stevenson, 2007).

In 1995, only 9% of American adults had accessed the Internet (Moore & Kearsley, 2005). By 2002, 66% of American adults were accessing the Internet from their home or workplace using a graphical Internet web browser (Moore & Kearsley, 2005). As the number of home and work computers with Internet access increased, online distance education courses using web-based instruction became viable (Bates, 2001).

Evolving Internet technology has prompted campuses to provide synchronous and asynchronous online instructional activities (Carter, 2008; Hwong, 2003; Su, 2006; Zhang, Zhao, Zhou, & Nunamaker, 2004). Asynchronous instruction frees students and instructors from the constraints of meeting at the same location and at the same time (Webb, Gill, & Poe, 2005). Blogs, on-demand video streaming, and discussion boards are considered asynchronous because participants can engage in and exchange ideas or information at different times (Tapscott & Williams, 2008).

Synchronous online instruction allows participants to exchange ideas and information at the same time (Meyer, 2002; Zhang, 2003). For example, online chat sessions and live audio or video-conferencing allow participants to engage in and exchange ideas in "real time" (Dron, 2007; Zhang, 2003). Most campuses offer students a mix of both asynchronous and synchronous online instruction (Moore & Kearsey, 2005). They range from several blended forms to completely online distance education courses. Campus leaders decide the various degrees of online distance education courses they will offer on their campuses (Bates, 2001).

For example, a campus may offer hybrid courses. Campuses offering hybrid courses blend face-to-face or traditional instruction with online instruction. Students enrolled in a hybrid course reduce traditional classroom instruction time because a portion of the course is presented using online instruction. Highland Community College offers hybrid courses (HCC, 2006). In their hybrid courses, at least 49% of the hybrid course's instructions can be presented using online instructional activities (HCC, 2006).

Campuses offering blended degree programs offer students a mixture of course delivery options. Their students may have options to attend a traditional, hybrid, or online course in order to complete their degree program. A blended campus offers students the opportunity to attend a course in a virtual or traditional classroom.

4

Within the virtual classrooms, students are allowed to select learning modules that employ e-learning technologies. For example, DeVry University offers courses in their degree programs that can be completed in either a virtual or traditional classroom (DeVry University, 2009).

Campuses offering online degree programs provide online instructional activities in virtual classrooms only. A student enrolled on an online campus can only take courses in a virtual classroom. Students do not have an option of attending a course in a traditional classroom; however, they can select multiple online instructional activities to assist them with learning course material. For example, the University of Phoenix offers degree programs that can only be completed using online instructions in virtual classrooms (University of Phoenix, 2009).

In addition to Internet technology providing a means for online instructions, new mobile devices with Internet capabilities have evolved (Lester & Piore, 2004; Tapscott & Williams, 2008). Mobile Internet technology provides a means for course instructions to be accessed on handheld devices (Tech & Learning, 2009). The ability to access online instructional activities using mobile devices offers students and educators a new paradigm of technology-enabled education (Tech & Learning, 2009). Research indicates self-directed learning improves when mobile technology is effectively integrated to give the learner the feel of personal or one-to-one contact with their educator (Tech & Learning, 2009).

Statement of the Problem

Leaders around the world and in all industries are facing a new kind of challenge - coping with rapid changes within their business environment due to Internet technology (Dess & Picken, 2000; Senge, 1997). Because Internet technology has provided campuses a means to offer flexible and convenient distance education (Webb, Gill, & Poe, 2005), adult learners are enrolling on campuses that offer online distance education courses. However, at least 21% of these adult learners are dropping out of online classes because they want a more engaging online learning experience (Kim & Bonk, 2006; Schaffhauser, 2009).

The convergence of competition, cost, technology, and new consumer demands have suggested that there are different rules for engaging students (Beaudoin, 2002). Empirical studies suggest that employing multiple e-learning technologies in an online distance education course can enhance teaching (Zhang, 2003). However, distance education leaders must consider their competitors, costs, and consumer demands while accomplishing their mission in a rapidly changing environment due to evolving Internet technology (Beaudoin, 2002). The problem is deciding which e-learning technologies to employ that will engage students in online distance education courses while competing in a rapidly changing industry due to evolving Internet technology.

Purpose of the Study

The purpose of this quantitative study was to compare two types of adult learners – adult learners enrolled on an online campus and adult learners enrolled on blended campuses – and their selection of e-learning technologies to engage their instructor, course content, and other learners in a virtual classroom.

Rationale

Beaudoin (2002) points out that online distance education should be central to an educational institution's strategic plan for success in the new global marketplace. Learning is shifting from traditional classrooms to homes, offices, (Zhang, 2003) and anywhere else students have Internet access (Harriman, 2004). Given the significance of e-learning technologies employed by campuses, the increase in enrollment of adult learners in online distance education courses, and the high drop-out rates of online students, a fuller understanding of the links between e-learning technologies used by adult learners to engage instructors, course content, and other learners is warranted.

Research Questions

In this study, the dependent variables are the counts of different e-learning technologies used by adult learners. There are two types of adult learners – the adult learner enrolled on an online campus and adult learners enrolled on a blended campus. However, both types of adult learners obtain online instructions in the same virtual course room.

The independent variables are e-learning technologies. E-learning technologies consist of e-learning media and devices. E-learning tools are hardware devices that allow learners to access synchronous and asynchronous online instructional activities (Paulus, 2003). For example, personal computers, laptops, netbooks, portable media players, and Smartphones are hardware devices that can be used by learners to access online instructional activities (Harriman, 2004; Tech & Learning, 2009).

E-learning media are online synchronous and asynchronous software learners use to engage their instructor, course content, and other learners (Dron, 2007). For example, discussion boards, e-mail, instant messaging, text messaging, blogs, chat sessions, e-books, and multimedia presentations allow learners to engage their instructor, course content, and other learners (Carter, 2008; Hwong, 2003; Su, 2006; Webb, Gill, & Poe, 2005; Zhang, Zhao, Zhou, & Nunamaker, 2004). E-learning technologies used in web-based instruction are measured by usage tracking (Carter, 2008; Hwong, 2003; & Yu, 1998). The research questions for the study are as follows.

1. What Internet devices are adult learners using to access their instructor, course content, and other learners? See hypothesis H1.

2. What e-learning media are adult learners using to engage their instructor, course content, and other learners? See hypothesis H2.

3. Is there a difference between the counts of e-learning technologies used by adult learners enrolled on a blended campus and adult learners enrolled on

an online campus when engaging their instructor, course content, and other learners in the same virtual classroom? See hypothesis H3.

Significance of the Study

This study added to the body of knowledge by expanding on research to explore online distance education. Most researchers (Ally, 2008; Bates, 2001; Charlson, 2006; Moore & Kearsley, 2005; Percival & Muirhead, 2009; Rovai, 2003; Singh, 2003; Tapscott & Williams, 2008; Webb, Gill, & Poe, 2005; Zhang, 2003; Zhang, Zhao, Zhou, & Nunamaker, 2004) have investigated the use of Internet technology in distance education. Although theories have been developed about e-learning technologies used in online distance education (Ally, 2008; Bates, 2001; & Zhang, 2003), there is no research about adult learners enrolled on two different campuses (online and blended) interacting in the same virtual classroom.

Several researchers (Charlson, 2006; Paul, 1990; Percival & Muirhead, 2009; Webb, Gill, & Poe, 2005) focused on comparing course outcomes of campuses that provided students different distance education opportunities (distance, traditional, or hybrid) (Beaudoin, 2002). This study provides campus administrators with comparative insights on the e-learning technologies used by adult learners enrolled on two different campuses (online and blended) sharing the same virtual classroom.

Definition of Terms

Adult Learner. For the purpose of this study, is defined as someone over the

9

age of twenty-five who is employed full, or part-time, or who has family and community responsibilities, and is motivated to attend college (Kasworm, 2003).

Asynchronous Media. For the purpose of this study, asynchronous media are Internet collaboration software employed by students that allow students to engage instructors, course content, and other learners at times convenient to them (Zhang, 2003). For example, a discussion board is an asynchronous medium because interaction with the instructor and other learners occur at different times.

Blended Campus. For the purpose of this study, a blended campus offers courses within their degree programs that can be completed in either a virtual, traditional or hybrid classroom (Webb, Gill & Poe, 2005).

Blended Program. For the purpose of this study, a blended program offers students the ability to complete courses in their degree program in a virtual, traditional, or hybrid classrooms (Bates, 2001).

Chat Rooms. A chat room is a web page that enables synchronous interaction using text. For example, a student can enter a group chat room and communicate with their team mates in real time (Bates, 2001).

Discussion Board. A discussion board is Internet collaboration software that allows students to interact asynchronously on a web page (Turoff, Howard, & Discenza, 2005).

Distance Education. Distance education is a formal educational process in which the majority of instructions in the course occur when students and instructors are not in the same place (Southern Association of Colleges and Schools, 2006).

E-book. An e-book is a digital media (electronic book) in portable document file (pdf) format that is accessed from a website. Its contents are equivalent to a conventional book (Percival & Muirhead, 2009).

E- Learning Medium. For the purpose of this study, an e-learning medium is synchronous or asynchronous web medium employed by learners to engage instructors, course content, and other learners (Zhang, D., 2003). For example, a web-based discussion board in a virtual classroom is an asynchronous e-learning medium.

E-Learning Module. For the purpose of this study, an e-learning module is one unit of instruction presented using e-learning media (Zhang, D., 2003). For example, an on-demand web-based multimedia presentation presented about the topic of study is an e-learning module.

E-Learning Devices. For the purpose of this study, e-learning devices allow learners to access e-learning media (Paulus, 2003). For example, a personal computer or netbook with Internet access allows learners to access e-learning modules in an online distance education course.

E-Learning Technology. For the purpose of this study, e-learning technology is e-learning media and tools employed by learners to engage the instructor, course content, and other learners (Zhang, 2003). For example, an e-learning media would be an on-demand multimedia presentation. The e-learning tool would be the portable media player used to access the on-demand multimedia presentation.

11

Engagement. For the purpose of this study, engagement is the amount of interaction a learner has with the instructor, course content, and other learners (Siemens, 2007).

Hybrid Course. A hybrid course uses a mixture of online and traditional instructions while requiring learners to report to a traditional classroom at sometime during the course (Bates, 2001).

Instant Messaging. Instant messaging is a form of Internet-based real-time communication between two or more people using text. For example, a student can interact with their instructor or other learners by selecting their name and typing a message.

Instructional Activity. For the purpose of this study, an instructional activity is an educational event that helps learners understand the content better and enhances their engagement in learning (Su, 2006). For example, feedback from the instructor or other learners is an instructional activity.

Mobile Learning. For the purpose of this study, mobile learning (m-learning) is web-based instruction presented on handheld Internet devices (Harriman, 2004). For example, e-Readers, palmtops (handheld personal computers with Internet capabilities), smart phones (mobile phones with personal computer and/or Internet capabilities), and portable media players can be used to access online course information.

Mobile E-Learning Tools. For the purpose of this study, a mobile e-learning tool is a portable computing device with Internet access that has a display screen with touch-input capabilities and/or a miniature keyboard (Traylor, 2009). For example, a laptop, portable media player, and Smartphones are examples of mobile e-learning tools.

On-Demand Multimedia Presentation. For the purpose of this study, on-demand multimedia presentation is an audio, video, or combination of both audio and video stream viewed over the Internet or that can be downloaded to be listened to when not connected to the Internet (Turoff, Howard, & Discenza, 2005; Waits & Lewis, 2003).

Online Campus. For the purpose of this study, an online campus offers distance education courses only in virtual classrooms using web-based instructions (Ally, 2008).

Online Degree Programs. For the purpose of this study, an online degree program offers students the ability to earn a degree using only web-based instructions (Singh, O'Donoghue, & Betts, 2002).

Online Distance Education. Online distance education is when the learner is at a distance from their instructor, uses some form of Internet technology to access learning materials, and uses Internet technology to interact with their instructor and other learners (Ally, 2008).

Synchronous Media. For the purpose of this study, synchronous learning media are web media used by students to engage with instructors, course content, and other learners at the same time (real time) (Zhang, 2003). For example, students meet in a group chat room in order to interact with instructors and other students.

Self-Directed Learning. Self directed learning is learning in which the learner initiates and takes responsibility for learning (Knowles, et al., 2005).

Text Messaging. For the purpose of this study, text messaging is interacting by sending short messages from mobile handheld devices. For example, a learner can send a short message to their instructor using a PDA.

Traditional Classroom. For the purpose of this study, a traditional classroom is a room in a building where teacher and students meet to discuss and learn course information (Kreitzer, 1999).

Traditional Student. For the purpose of this study, a traditional student is between the age of 18 and 24, attending college full time, and is financially dependent (National Center for Educational Statistics, 2007).

Virtual Classroom. For the purpose of this study, a virtual classroom is one section of multiple sections of a course offered by a campus that allows students to interact with their instructor, course content, and other learners employing synchronous and asynchronous e-learning media (Hansen, 2001).

Virtual Course Room. For the purpose of this study, a virtual course room is all sections of a virtual course offered by a campus that allows students to interact with their instructor, course content, and other learners employing synchronous and asynchronous e- learning media (Hansen, 2001).

14

Web. The Web is the computer network consisting of a collection of Internet sites that offer text, graphics, sound, and animation resources through the use of hypertext transfer protocol (HTTP) (Tapscott & Williams, 2008).

Web-based Instruction (WBI). For the purpose of this study, web-based instruction occurs in virtual classrooms where learners control which e-learning technologies to employ in order to engage instructors, course content, and other learners (Sims, 1999).

Web Conferencing. For the purpose of this study, web conferencing is an audio or video synchronous broadcast in which the presenter and audience are communicating using video-conferencing software (Turoff, Howard, & Discenza, 2005; Waits & Lewis, 2003).

Web Media. For the purpose of this study, web media properties are learner controlled modules that provide a means for communicating using asynchronous and synchronous Internet technology (Yu, 1998). For example, web media properties are discussion boards, streaming video and audio, and e-mail systems.

Assumptions and Limitations

The major assumption of this study is that the respondents were honest in the information that they provided and were not influenced by others. In addition, the researcher assumed that surveying adult learners in one virtual course room will provide data about e-learning technologies used by adult learners enrolled on two different campuses (online and blended) to engage their instructor, course content, and other learners. Other assumptions are the adult learner was fully aware of their needs; could accurately assess the specific learning required; was motivated enough to engage in any learning required; and was motivated enough to engage in any learning needed (Knowles, et al., 2005). In other words, it was assumed that the adult learner is a self-directed learner.

One limitation of this quantitative study was data was retrieved from only one university that has an online campus and four blended campuses. In addition, data was only collected from adult learners who had taken the same graduate course at the online campus. Therefore, this study may not be applicable to all campuses or online distance education courses.

Another limitation is technology changes rapidly. By the time this research was completed, changes in handheld Internet technology had occurred.

Theoretical Framework

WBI occurs in virtual classrooms where learners employ e-learning technologies in order to engage their instructor, course content, and other learners (Bates, 1995; Carter, 2008; Hwong, 2003; Sims, 1999; Su, 2006; Webb, Gill & Poe, 2005; Yu, 1998; Zhang, Zhao, Zhou, & Nunamaker, 2004). In this quantitative study, the dependent variables are the counts of different e-learning technologies used by adult learners enrolled on blended and online campuses. The independent variables are the e-learning technologies adult learners can use to access and engage online instructional activities in a virtual classroom.

E-learning technologies consist of e-learning media and devices. E-learning devices are personal computers, laptops, netbooks, portable media players, and Smartphones. E-learning media are e-mail, instant messaging, text messaging, chat sessions, e-books, and multimedia presentations. Yu (1998) believed that counting the use of e-learning technologies in a virtual classroom can reflect user engagement.

Summary

The adult learner population is growing both in number and in proportion to the traditional student population (National Center for Educational Statistics, 2007). Most of these adult learners are enrolling on campuses that offer online distance education courses. Adult learners' reason for enrolling in an online distance education course is a desire to fit acquiring an education into a busy schedule that includes family, community, and careers.

The university in this study provides online distance education degree

17

programs to two types of adult learners – adult learners enrolled on an online campus and adult learners enrolled on blended campuses. The online campus provides web-based instructions in virtual classrooms for university students enrolled on their blended and online campuses. This study intends to compare adult learners (enrolled on blended campuses and one online campus) use of e-learning technologies to engage their instructor, course content, and other learners.

Organization of the Remainder of the Study

The information in this study is organized by chapters. Chapter 2 contains a literature review of the Internet; facilitating learning; online distance education; online and blended campuses; and the adult learners. Chapter 2 concludes with a discussion of variables that have been used in previous research to measure learners' e-learning technologies use. Chapter 3 contains the methodology, procedures, and data analysis of the study. Chapter 4 contains the findings and analysis. Chapter 5 contains the summary of findings from data analysis, the conclusion derived from the findings, a discussion related to the study, and a recommendation for further study.

CHAPTER 2. LITERATURE REVIEW

Overview

Online distance education courses are being employed by campuses to deliver course instruction (Traylor, 2009). Since online distance education courses permit learners to acquire instruction at a time and place convenient to them, adult learners are enrolling in these courses hoping to fit acquiring an education into their busy lives (Charlson, 2006). However, campus administrators are confronted with between 40% to 80% of these adult learners dropping out of online classes (Tyler-Smith, 2006) while 21% of these adult learners are pleading for richer and more engaging online learning experiences (Kim & Bonk, 2006; Schaffhauser, 2009).

This chapter presents literature related to e-learning technologies offered in online distance education courses that may be used by adult learners to engage their instructor, course content, and other learners. Using past studies and relevant literature, this chapter is organized into five categories: (a) Introduction to the Internet, (b) Facilitating Learning (c) Adult Learners, (d) Online Distance Education, and (e) Online and Blended Campuses. The chapter concludes with a discussion of variables that have been used in previous research to measure learners' Internet usage.

Introduction to the Internet

In 1958, President Dwight D. Eisenhower created the Advanced Research Projects Agency (ARPA) as a direct response to the Soviet Union launch of the first man-made satellite (Sputnik). In 1960, ARPA set up a network that linked together computers of the armed forces, universities, and defense contractors running four different operating systems on their computers (Lester & Piore, 2004). They called their network ARPANET.

In 1971, Intel invented the microprocessor. In 1975, the first personal computer came onto the market. In 1976, ARPANET connected to the Packet Radio Network (PRNET). A PRNET connects computers through radio transmitters and receivers instead of sending data across telephone lines (Caprone, 1990). In 1977, technicians joined the Satellite Network (SATNET) to ARPANET and PRNET. They called the connection between multiple networks inter-networking or the INTERNET for short.

In the mid 1980s, the National Science Foundation (NSF) developed a network of five supercomputer centers which connected universities and research organizations (Moore & Kearsley, 2005). This network was employed by individuals to interact using e-mail and electronic bulletin boards. Individuals were also able to transfer data files and access libraries using terminals (Charlson, 2006). At this time, the Internet was a dark place in which white, red, or green text on a black screen was transmitted from one terminal or computer to another terminal or computer.

In 1985, The National Technology University, an accredited online university, began offering graduate courses and degrees in engineering (Kreitzer, 1999). Their courses were taught by faculty from several universities by satellite uplink to universities, businesses, and government agencies (Moore & Kearsey, 2005). Because NTU offered a selection of courses from a large number of universities, prospective adult learners and organizations could decide which university's course they would enroll in. This required members of this consortium to compete against each other to offer the best quality courses for their customers (Moore & Kearsey, 2005). As a result, students and organizations began to dictate which courses were marketable (Moore & Kearsey, 2005).

The first two-way video-conferencing was expensive and required classrooms to connect to one another using a compression device called codec located in a personal computer (Charlson, 2006). In 1986, Michael Moore of Penn State University used a T1 line to implement the first graduate course delivered at a distance using two-way video-conferencing (Kreitzer, 1999). According to Moore and Kearsley (2005), two-way video-conferencing became faster, easier, and less costly with the development of fiber-optic telephone lines that displayed video on personal computers between locations.

In the 1990s, the Online Campus of New York Institute of Technology began offering entire degrees via the Internet (Moore & Kearsley, 2005). In addition, Penn State University began offering a graduate degree in Adult Education via the Internet.

In 1993, a graphical Internet web browser, Mosaic, allowed documents to be accessed from a distance using different types of computers, software, operational systems, and screen resolutions. This gave educators a new method for delivering courses. Courses could be delivered using previous e-learning media (e-mails, bulletin boards, and file transfer) as well as employing discussion boards, streaming video, video-conferencing, and electronic slide presentations (Scott, 2005).

In 1995, only 9% of American adults had accessed the Web (Moore & Kearsley, 2005). By the year 2002, 66% of American adults were accessing the Internet from their home or workplace (Moore & Kearsley, 2005). As the number of home and work computers with Internet access increased and Internet software evolved, various e-learning modules using synchronous and asynchronous media developed (Bates, 2001).

Facilitating Learning

Interaction and collaboration have been identified as the fundamental building blocks for facilitating learning (Bates, 2005; Carter, 2008; Garrison & Anderson, 2003). The constructivist approach stresses that all knowledge is context bound, people make personal meaning of their learning experiences, and learning cannot be separated from the context in which it is used (Carter, 2008; Larson & Alesandrini, 2002). This means that new knowledge must be related to old knowledge in order for learners to retain and use it (Rogers, 1946; Siemens, 2007).

The constructivist approach for an effective online learning environment are learner-centered, knowledge-centered, and assessment-centered (Rovai, 2004). The learner-centered approach places the learner at the center of the learning process and takes into consideration learners' background knowledge and beliefs (Siemens, 2007). Carl Rogers (1946) conceptualized a learner-centered approach to education. First, he hypothesized that a person cannot teach another person directly; a person can only facilitate learning. Secondly, a person learns those things they perceive are important in order to maintain and enhance themselves. Thirdly, a person may only be able to acquire knowledge that is inconsistent with their experiences in a supportive environment in which the student is responsible for the learning (Rogers, 1946). Lastly, the educational environment that most effectively promotes significant learning is nonthreatening; grounded in facts, allows the person to evaluate facts in multiple ways, and allows the person to test their assumptions and concepts with reality (Rogers, 1946).

Knowledge-centered learning highlights the importance of the role of the instructor to set the course for learning (Riel, 2000). Knowledge-centered learning provides learners with opportunities to develop critical thinking skills through self-reflection and thought processes (Siemens, 2007). In a knowledge-centered learning environment, the instructor introduces facts, ideas, concepts, and principles to the learner in a timely manner and in a way that that makes sense to the learner (Riel, 2000).

The assessment-centered approach to learning provides multiple opportunities for formative and summative feedback from the instructor and peers on the learner's progress (Siemens, 2007). This requires active engagement from the learner and continuous feedback from the instructor and other learners (Eisenbach, Golich, & Curry, 1998). Formative and summative feedback enables the learner to take responsibility for their learning and enhances the quality of their learning experience (Eisenbach, et al., 1998). For this reason, many educators (Palloff & Pratt, 1999; Moore & Kearsley, 2005; Berg, 1999; Zhang, 2003) believe that interaction is a critical element for a quality online education.

Online interaction and collaboration occur in virtual classrooms that allow learners to decide which e-learning technologies they will employ to engage in online instructional activities (Dron, 2007). A virtual classroom provides an environment in which learners take responsibility and control of their learning through negotiating meaning, diagnosing misconceptions, and challenging accepted beliefs (Bates, 2005). The ultimate goal of learning is the development of higher-order thinking skills (Dron, 2007). To develop these skills, learners need to frequently engage with others in a social environment that encourages critical thinking and considers diverse points of view (Dewey, 1996). Palloff and Pratt (1999) view learning as an active process that requires learners to engage their instructor, course material, and other learners.

The Adult Learner

An adult learner is someone who is responsible for their own life (Knowles, Horton, & Swanson, 2005), over the age of twenty-five, is employed full or part-time or has community responsibilities, and is motivated to attend college (Kasworm, 2003). Adult learners' orientation to learning is life-centered (Roberson, 2004). Adult learners enroll in a degree program in order to earn a degree that will enable them to acquire a promotion, new position, or new career (Compton, Cox, & Laanan, 2006; Berg, 2005).

Adult learners are motivated to learn to satisfy a need (Knowles, et al. 2005). Adult learners have a deep need to be self-directing (Lindeman, 1989). In addition, adult learners can learn inside and outside a formal classroom (Wickett, 2005). Today, women make up the majority of adult learners (Compton, Cox, & Laanan, 2006; Berg, 2005). Adult learners have different needs than traditional learners (Berg, 2005). For example, adult learners may need to work full or part-time while pursuing a degree.

Adults learn best in informal, comfortable, flexible, and nonthreatening settings (Knowles, et.al. 2005). Knowles itemized five conditions that must be met in order for adult learners to succeed.

1. Adult learners must know why the learning event is important.

2. Adult learners must be seen as capable of self-direction.

3. Adult learners must be able to share experiences related to the learning event.

4. Adult learners must be ready to learn.

5. Adult learners are motivated to learn by life situations.

Adult learners may worry about their children at home, their partners, and their careers (Berg, 2005). They seek educational opportunities that will allow them to fit acquiring education into their schedule (Charlson, 2006; Hagedorn, 2005). For this reason, most adult learners are likely to enroll in an online course with hopes of fitting an education into their busy lives (Compton, Cox, & Laanan, 2006; National Center for Educational Statistics, 2007). However, adult learners are dropping out of online classes while pleading for richer and more engaging online learning experiences (Kim & Bonk, 2006; Schaffhauser, 2009). Financial challenges, life events, health issues, and lack of personal motivation are other reasons adult learners drop out of an online course (Schaffhauser, 2009).

Self-Directed Learning

Adult learners have a deep need to be self-directing (Lindeman, 1989). Tough's (1982) linear model of self-directed learning assumes that well-planned learning events should allow learners to move through a series of steps to reach their learning goals. In self-directed learning, the learner takes the initiative and the responsibility for learning (Knowles, et al., 2005). Individuals select, manage, and assess their own learning activities, which can be pursued at any time, in any place, through any means (Singh, 2003). There are many different kinds of self-directed learning programs and many ways to deliver them. Online distance education is one delivery method which allows learners to take initiative for their learning.

In the instructional model of self-directed learning, the best learning comes from skillful integration of self-directed learning by adult learners and formal instructional programs (Knowles, 1980). One concept of self-directed learning is self-teaching (Knowles, et.al. 2005). The assumption of self-teaching is learners are capable of taking control of the mechanics and techniques of teaching themselves a particular subject. Another conception of self-directed learning is a learner can assume ownership of their learning and take control of the goals and purposes of learning (p. 186).

An adult learner who is experienced with the subject matter and has strong self-directed learning skills will become frustrated by too much direction (Knowles, et.al. 2005). A student who is inexperienced with the subject and has poorly developed self-directed learning skills is likely to be intimidated by the many learning alternatives (p. 187). In addition, a student with strong self-directed learning skills and inexperience with the subject matter may want direction from the instructor.

The adult learner population is growing both in number and in proportion to the traditional student population (National Center for Educational Statistics, 2007). Most of these adult learners enroll in online distance education courses hoping they will be able to fit acquiring a degree into their busy lives (Kasworm, 2003). However,

between 40% to 80% drop out of online classes (Tyler-Smith, 2006) and 21% are

pleading for a more engaging online learning experience (Kim & Bonk, 2006;

Schaffhauser, 2009).

Online Distance Education

Distance education is a formal educational process in which the instructions in

the course occur when students and instructors are not in the same place (Shale &

Gomes, 1998; Southern Association of Colleges and Schools, 2006; National Center

for Educational Statistics, 2007). Online distance education occurs when the learner

is at a distance from their instructor and employs e-learning technologies to engage

their instructor, course content, and other learners (Ally, 2008).

Online distance education will consist of one or more of the following

elements: a web site; e-learning modules consisting of web-based asynchronous and

synchronous media; course material posted by the instructor; access to web-based

resources via links to other web sites, assessments, and e-books or articles (Bates,

1995). The web site normally contains orientation to the course, course objectives;

list of course contents, course schedule, and assignment questions (p. 138). The web

site may allow instructors to post announcements or documents to enhance the

course. The web site will consist of online instructional activities consisting of

readings, online student activities, assessments, and means of providing feedback (p.

138).

E-Learning Modules

A medium is the form in which information is communicated (Thill & Bovee, 2007). E-learning modules consist of synchronous and asynchronous online media software that allows learners to engage their instructor, course content, and other learners (Dron, 2007). Online media can be in the form of e-mail, instant messaging, web sites, text messaging, and blogs (Thill & Bovee, 2007). Online multimedia is Internet software that communicates information using text, illustrations, photographs, narration, music, animation, and film clips (Capron, 1997).

Blogs, on-demand video streaming, and discussion boards are considered asynchronous because participants can engage in and exchange ideas or information at different times. Synchronous online learning activities allow participants to exchange ideas and information at the same time (Zhang, 2003). For example, online chat sessions, instant messaging, and live audio or video-conferencing are examples of synchronous communication.

Learner Engagement

Learner engagement is the amount of interaction a learner has with their instructor, course content, and other learners (Siemens, 2007). Students engage instructors and other learners by posting on discussion boards, attending faculty live chat sessions, instant messaging their instructor during faculty office hours, viewing faculty recorded chat sessions, viewing faculty comments and announcement postings, and e-mailing their instructor and classmates (Dron, 2007). In addition, students receive online instruction using streaming media (Zhang, 2003). An on-demand stream is asynchronous and is stored on a server to be transmitted at the user's request (Ally, 2003). Live streams are synchronous and available at the time of the event or presentation (Zhang, Zhao, Zhou, & Nunamaker, 2004). Most campuses offer students a mix of both asynchronous and synchronous communication technology in the delivery of online instructions (Moore & Kearsey, 2005).

A learner's engagement in an online distance education course is identified by their interaction with the instructors, course content, and other learners (Siemens, 2007). Garrison and Anderson's (2003) Community of Inquiry model highlights three forms of interactions - student-instructor, student-content, and student-student. The primary focus of these interactions are to provide increased control to learners, adapt the program based on learner feedback, and to facilitate a range of participation, communication opportunities that contribute to meaningful learning experiences, and self-reflection (Riel, 2000; Sims, 1999).

There are several e-learning technologies that can be employed to engage the learner (Ally, 2008). Learners use synchronous and asynchronous online instructional activities to engage their instructor, course content, and other learners (Carter, 2008; Hwong, 2003; Su, 2006; Zhang, 2003). Since a variety of synchronous and asynchronous online instructional activities can be employed to engage the learner (Zhang, 2003), campus leaders are struggling with deciding which synchronous and asynchronous online instructional activities will allow them to complete their mission while engaging learners (Beaudoin, 2002).

Online and Blended Campuses

Beaudoin (2002) pointed out that online distance education should be central to an educational institution's strategic plan for success in the new global marketplace. Before deciding to implement new processes to meet an objective, leaders of online organizations must consider the mission of the organization (Levitt & March, 1988) and identify the organization's core competencies (Nevis, DiBella, & Gould, 1995). One core competency of an online campus is their use of e-learning technologies. Online and blended campuses offer varying means for meeting the instructional needs of their learners (Bates, 1995).

An online campus offers students the ability to earn a degree using only e-learning technologies to engage in online instructional activities (Singh, O'Donoghue, & Betts, 2002). Campuses offering online degree programs provide instructions in a virtual classroom. A virtual classroom is where learners engage their instructor, course content and other learners using online synchronous and asynchronous media (Hansen, 2001). This frees the instructor and learners from meeting in the same location. Learners are able to access online instructional activities at any time and place they have Internet access. For example, University of Phoenix offers degrees that can be completed entirely using web-based instructions.

University of Phoenix offers associate, bachelor, and master degrees in business.

A blended campus provides courses in their degree program that can be taken in virtual classrooms, traditional classrooms, or by means of both online and traditional instructions (Webb, Gill, & Poe, 2005). For example, AIU-Atlanta, University of North Carolina at Chapel Hill, and North Carolina State University in Raleigh offer the learner a choice between taking a course within their academic programs in a virtual or traditional classroom. A traditional classroom is a room in a building where instructor and learners meet face-to-face to engage in instructional activities (Kreitzer, 1999). A hybrid course uses a mixture of online and traditional instructions while requiring learners to report to a traditional classroom at sometime during the course (Bates, 2001). Blended campuses give learners the option of taking a course in a virtual or traditional classroom.

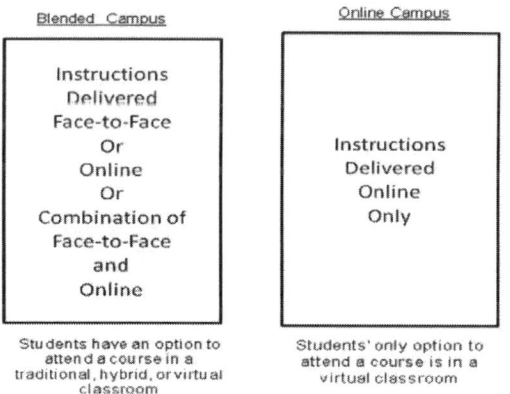

Figure 1. Two types of campuses – blended and online designed by B. Smith for this dissertation.

Internet technology enables institutions to enroll learners beyond their city, state, or national borders (Charlson, 2006). In the past twenty years, for-profit web-based degree granting institutions of higher learning have increased in number by 112% while as many as 200 traditional colleges have ceased to exist (Ruch, 2001). At the same time, more accredited traditional educational institutions offer distance education via the Internet (Charlson, 2006). It is significant to note that many of the institutions adopting online distance learning are among the most well-established and highly regarded in the country. For example North Carolina State University in Raleigh, North Carolina as well as the University of North Carolina in Chapel Hill, North Carolina offer accredited online distance education courses.

There are over fifty colleges offering online distance education degrees (associate, bachelor, masters, and/or doctoral). For example, Anthem College Online offers associate and bachelor degrees in technology, healthcare, business, graphic design and animation, and criminal justice. Benedictine University offers online Master of Business Administration (MBA) general degrees as well as MBAs with healthcare and international business concentrations.

In the year 2000, 84% of public universities, 83% of public 4-year colleges, and 70% of community colleges delivered course information using Internet technology (Moore & Kearsley, 2005). In addition, 53% of private universities and 35% of private four year colleges delivered course information using Internet technology (Moore & Kearsley, 2005). It is clear that online distance education will have a strong presence in the future of higher education (Singh, O'Donoghue, &

Betts, 2002).

According to Flint (2001), the method of instructional delivery (courses available on or off campus) indicates an institution's ability to be innovative in meeting the needs of their learners. When objectives are clear and consistent, defined by members of the college community, taken to heart by campus leaders, and invoked as guides for decision-making, colleges are generally more effective and efficient in meeting the needs of their online learners (Siemens, 2007).

Learners' Internet Use

Many researchers (Ally, 2008; Bates, 2001; Charlson, 2006; Moore & Kearsley, 2005; Percival & Muirhead, 2009; Rovai, 2003; Singh, 2003; Tapscott & Williams, 2008; Webb, Gill, & Poe, 2005; Zhang, 2003; Zhang, Zhao, Zhou, & Nunamaker, 2004) have investigated the use of Internet technology in distance education. Several researchers (Charlson, 2006; Paul, 1990; Percival & Muirhead, 2009; Su, 2006; Webb, Gill, & Poe, 2005) focus on comparing course outcomes of campuses that provided students different distance education opportunities (distance, traditional, or a mixture of both). All these researchers believe there is a need to develop a better understanding of the role of technology in distance education.

Two problems in the study of online distance education are the wide range of teaching strategies and various content areas (Carter, 2008; Charlson, 2006; Webb, Gill, & Poe, 2005). Several researchers believe that online distance education research needs to precede course-by-course because teaching strategies and technologies that fit in one course may not fit in another course (Carter, 2008; Charlson, 2006; Moore & Kearsley, 2005; Percival & Muirhead, 2009; Su, 2006; Webb, Gill, & Poe, 2005). For example, the Carter (2008) study assessed adult learners' engagement in an undergraduate History of Sports and Physical Education course that required students to interact using avatars in a Second Life virtual world. Su's (2006) study analyzed MBA students' experiences and technological preferences in their online distance education courses. The Webb, Gill, and Poe (2005) study compared the outcomes of interactions and learning outcomes of graduate students enrolled in a traditional, light online hybrid, heavy online hybrid, and pure online Management Information Systems (MIS) survey course.

Another issue with online distance education is the high drop-out rate across disciplines (Carter, 2008; Kim & Bonk, 2006; Schaffhauser, 2009; Su, 2006; Tyler-Smith, 2006). Many of the common factors often expressed by online learners that may lead to high attrition rates are lack of engagement with course content, limited opportunities for deliberation and discourse as well as a lack of social interaction among peers (Carter, 2008; Kim & Bonk, 2006; Moore & Kearsley, 2005; Schaffhauser, 2009; Su, 2006; Tyler-Smith, 2006). Additionally, feelings of isolation, frustration with course-related technical issues, and slow-to-respond technical support have also been cited as underlying reasons for high attrition in online courses (Barritt; 1998; Carter, 2008).

Researchers (Carter, 2008; 2009; Percival & Muirhead, 2009; Su, 2006; Webb, Gill, & Poe, 2005) have used mixed research methods to gather information about learner's demographics, technology experiences, engagement using technology, as well as adult learners' perception of the e-learning technologies employed. The findings in these studies have resulted in calls for further research in how to engage learners using Internet technology in different courses and on different campus types (Barritt,1998; Carter, 2008; Su, 2006; & Webb, Gill, & Poe, 2005). In online distance education studies, quantitative data was collected by administering survey instruments that were modified to count the use of e-learning technologies used in the course being studied (Carter, 2008; Hwong, 2003; Percival & Muirhead, 2009; Robinson, 2005; Su, 2006; & Webb, Gill, & Poe, 2005). Qualitative data was collected by researchers (Carter, 2008; Charlson, 2006; & Su, 2006) using interviews and open-end questions to explain the reasons for learners' choices of e-learning technologies.

This study followed the research of Hwong (2003) and Su (2006) and investigated variables in three categories: learner-instructor and learner-learner online interactions as well as Internet access. In addition to these variables, the current study will also include the variable student-content. These variables will be used to count e-learning technologies used by adult learners to engage their instructor, course content, and other learners in a virtual classroom.

Su's (2006) research investigated 188 MBA students use of synchronous and

36

asynchronous online instructional activities that promoted learner-instructor and learner-learner interactions. Su's (2006) research indicated that many educators (Palloff & Pratt, 1999; Moore & Kearsley, 2005; Berg, 1999; Zhang, 2003) believed that interaction is a critical element for a quality online education. However, Su's (2006) research also indicated that interaction does not naturally occur in a virtual classroom. The instructional design must incorporate learning opportunities that include flexible opportunities for learner-instructor and learner-learner interactions (Su, 2006).

In the virtual classroom, learning opportunities are instructional activities. Instructional activities are educational events that help students understand content better and enhances their engagement in learning (Su, 2006). Su scrutinized learners' preferences for engagement with instructors and other learners because learners are the ultimate recipients of online education (p.4). Su believed their voices should be heard and reflected in the course design process. He based this belief on Knowles' theory of andragogy which implies if adults are given enough control over their learning and if their needs are addressed, they can make the learning experience more meaningful for them (p. 5).

Learner-Instructor Online Interaction Variables

In learner-instructor interactions, the instructor serves as an expert and plans instructions that actively engage learners (Garrison & Anderson, 2003). Interaction between instructor and learner can take place employing synchronous and

37

asynchronous online media – discussion boards, faculty chat sessions, and faculty recorded lectures (Moore & Kearsley, 2005; Percival & Muirhead, 2009; Su, 2006; Webb, Gill, & Poe, 2005; & Zhang, Zhao, Zhou, & Nunamaker, 2004). For example, the instructor can respond to students' postings on a discussion board. In addition, the instructor can establish online office hours and invite learners to contact them using instant messaging software during their office hours. Also, instructors can use electronic slides to engage the learner during an online presentation about course material.

During a synchronous multimedia presentation, learners can communicate with their instructors at the time of the presentation. During an asynchronous multimedia presentation, the learner can send an e-mail to the instructor to ask questions about information discussed during the live presentation. The instructor's expert knowledge and experience with the topic and e-learning technology allows them to provide quality information and develop an effective plan for student-instructor interactions (Garrison & Anderson, 2003).

Su (2006) believed that instructors should promote a social presence, provide quality feedback, as well as engage in meaningful conversations. Based on strategies suggested by various online instructors, Su synthesized list of instructional activities used in online learner-instructor interactions are

- Use synchronous lectures that allow real-time questioning and responding

- Use asynchronous lectures that involve delayed questioning and responding

- Incorporate virtual office hours for individual synchronous consultation

- Participate in group-level discussions

- Participate in class-level discussions (p. 35).

Learner-Learner Online Interaction Variables

Learner-learner interaction is when learners engage their peers using synchronous and asynchronous media (Garrison & Anderson, 2003). As learners interact with other learners using synchronous and asynchronous discussion, "they are challenged to reflect on and re-evaluate their own understandings of the course material while considering the perspectives of their peers, thus developing social and critical thinking skills" (Siemens, 2007). Learners interact with other learners using discussion boards, chat rooms, and e-mail (Moore & Kearsley, 2005; Percival & Muirhead, 2009; Su, 2006; Webb, Gill, & Poe, 2005; & Zhang, Zhao, Zhou, & Nunamaker, 2004). Su synthesized list of instructional activities used in online learner-learner interactions are

- Small group (groups that consist of three to six learners) asynchronous discussion

- Class-level asynchronous discussions

- Synchronous chat discussions among learners

- Learners evaluate other learners' work and provide feedback

- Learners share information and resources (p. 36).

Su's (2006) study revealed that learners did not prefer class-level asynchronous discussion especially when the class size was large, repetitive postings were required, and rules and expectations were unclear. In general, online learners prefer to engage in both types of interactions – learner-instructor and learner-learner. The results of Su's (2006) research suggest the existence of other variables that may affect online interactions.

In Su's (2006) study, synchronous and asynchronous online instructional activities were grouped into two categories and measured counting the frequency of use. In order to obtain a clearer picture of learner usage, each synchronous and asynchronous activity will be measured. For example, some asynchronous media are e-mails, discussion boards, recorded chat sessions, and recorded multimedia presentations. Since a variety of synchronous and asynchronous learning media are used in the delivery of online learning (Hwong, 2003; Moore & Kearsley, 2005; Percival & Muirhead, 2009; Su, 2006; Webb, Gill, & Poe, 2005; Zhang, 2003; & Zhang, Zhao, Zhou, & Nunamaker, 2004), it seems appropriate to identify which specific e-learning media learners employ in a virtual classroom in order to decide where a campus' future information technology investments should be focused (Percival & Muirhead, 2009; Rovia, 2003).

Learner-Content Online Interaction Variables

Learner-content online interaction refers to the learners' engagement with course materials (Garrison & Anderson, 2003). This can be in the form of e-books, electronic articles, web pages, and multimedia presentations (Bates, 2005). To facilitate learner-content interactions, clear goals and learning expectations need to be presented; course content should be presented using various learning modules; and frequent opportunities for self-directed learning and constructive feedback should be employed (Garrison & Anderson, 2003). For example, providing students an e-book, an announcement on a web page, and multimedia presentation that covers the same content but allows the student to decide how to engage the course material to obtain a unit's objective would be considered a good method for providing learner-content engagement. In addition, instructor's comments to students about knowledge they acquired from the course content will enhance this learning experience (Sims, 1999). This current study expanded Su's (2006) study to include leaner-content interaction.

Accessing Online Instructional Activities

E-learning devices are computer hardware devices that allow students to access online instructional activities (Capron, 1998; Harriman, 2004; Tech & Learning, 2009). Examples of e-learning devices are laptops, netbooks, mobile handheld devices, and personal computers (Charlson, 2006). For example, the online university used in this study offers students the ability to access multimedia e-learning modules using a portable media player.

Portable media players allow students to download their on-demand classroom presentation in seconds and then view it at a time and place convenient for them. Examples of mobile e-learning tools are palmtops (handheld personal computers with possible Internet capabilities), smart phones (mobile phones with personal computer and/or Internet capabilities), and portable media players (mobile multimedia players with Internet capabilities). Research indicates self-directed learning improves when mobile e-learning tools are effectively integrated to give the learner a feel of personal or one-to-one engagement with their educator (Harriman, 2004; Tech & Learning, 2009).

In Hwong's (2003) quantitative study, online instructional activities were measured using a sixteen-item survey that counted the frequency of use of each online instructional activity. Each item consisted of a five-point rating scale: 1 = *never*, 2 = *rarely*, 3 = *sometimes*, 4 = *often*, 5 = *very often*. Summing of the scores for the 16 items produced a total score for learner usage. The total score ranged from 80 to 16, with 80 as the highest score and 16 as the lowest score. A high score indicated a high level of engagement (p. 39).

Quantitative data analysis was based on 128 college students and was conducted using Statistical Package for the Social Sciences (SPSS). Both descriptive and inferential statistics were applied. Percentage and frequency counts were used to describe Internet usage and engagement. The calculation of means was used to determine respondent's holistic level of Internet usage. The holistic level of Internet

42

usage in Hwong's (2003) study was 3.07. Hwong's (2003) results were presented in tables.

Hwong's (2003) study was expanded in this study to include Internet devices used to access online learning activities. As new Internet technologies come into existence, campuses seek ways to incorporate these technologies into their course delivery (Kreitzer, 1999). The latest Internet technologies are handheld mobile devices (Lester & Piore, 2004). The ability to interact using mobile e-learning devices offers learners and educators a new paradigm of technology-enabled education (Harriman, 2004; Tech & Learning, 2009). The current study investigated mobile devices that allow learners to access synchronous and asynchronous online instructional activities.

Summary

Currently, various online instructional activities are being employed by campuses to deliver course instruction (Traylor, 2009). Adult learners are enrolling in online distance education courses hoping to fit acquiring an education into their busy lives (Charlson, 2006). However, administrators are confronted with adult learners dropping out of online classes while pleading for richer and more engaging online learning experiences (Kim & Bonk, 2006).

Although theories have been developed about e-learning technologies used in online distance education courses (Ally, 2008; Bates, 2001; & Zhang, 2003), there is no research about adult learners enrolled on two different campuses (online and blended) interacting in the same virtual classroom. Researchers (Carter, 2008; Charlson, 2006; Moore & Kearsley, 2005; Percival & Muirhead, 2009; Su, 2006; Webb, Gill, & Poe, 2005) believe that online distance education research needs to precede course-by-course because teaching strategies and technologies that fit in one course may not fit in another course. In addition, there is little research on adult learners' usage of mobile devices to access online instructional activities. Given the significance of e-learning technologies employed by campuses, the increase in enrollment of adult learners in online distance education courses, and the high drop-out rates of online learners, a fuller understanding of the links between e-learning technologies used by adult learners to engage instructors, course content, and other learners is warranted.

CHAPTER 3. METHODOLOGY

Research Design

This chapter describes the investigative approach used in conducting the study, as well as the setting, instrumentation, data collection method, and analytical procedures. The purpose of this descriptive quantitative study was to compare two types of adult learners (those enrolled on blended campuses and those enrolled on an online campus) employment of e-learning technologies to engage their instructor, course content, and other learners in a virtual classroom. The investigative procedure entails examining two samples of students in one setting and involves comparing e-learning media and tools employed in a virtual classroom.

The campus in this study provides web-based instructions for students enrolled on a university's blended and online campus. Both types of students, those enrolled on an online and blended campus, attend courses in the same virtual classrooms. The question is whether or not these adult learners employ the same e-learning technologies to engage the instructor, course content, and other learners in the virtual classroom.

This study's research questions and hypotheses are listed below.

1. What Internet devices are adult learners using to access their instructor, course content, and other learners?

Ho1. There are no statistical differences in the number of adult learners using different types of Internet devices to access their instructor, course content, and other learners.

Ha1: There is a statistical difference in the number of adult learners using different types of Internet devices to access their instructor, course content, and other learners.

2. What e-learning media are adult learners using to engage their instructor, course content, and other learners?

Ho2. There are no statistical differences in the number of adult learners using different types of e-learning media to access their instructor, course content, and other learners.

Ha2. There is a statistical difference in the number of adult learners using different types of e-learning media to access their instructor, course content, and other learners.

3. Is there a difference between the counts of e-learning technologies used by adult learners enrolled on a blended campus and adult learners enrolled on an online campus when engaging their instructor, course content, and other learners in the same virtual classroom?

Ho3. There are no statistical differences in the number of adult learners enrolled on a blended campus and adult learners enrolled on an online campus using different types of e-learning technologies to access their instructor, course content, and other learners.

Ha3. There are statistical differences in the number of adult learners enrolled on a blended campus and adult learners enrolled on an online campus using different types of e-learning technologies to access their instructor, course content, and other learners.

Sample

This quantitative study explored whether there is a difference in the employment of e-learning devices and e-learning media by two types of adult learners (adult learners enrolled on blended campuses and adult learners enrolled on an online campus) engaging their instructor, course content, and other learners in the same virtual classroom. The adult learner is someone over the age of twenty-five who is employed full-time, part-time, or has family and community responsibilities, and is motivated to attend college (Kasworm, 2003).

The target population consisted of adult learners who have participated in the same graduate course on an online campus. Su's (2006) study analyzed MBA students' usage and technological preferences in their MBA distance education courses. Hwong (2003) survey identified students' Internet usage on one campus. Researchers (Carter, 2008; Charlson, 2006; Moore & Kearsley, 2005; Percival & Muirhead, 2009; Su, 2006; Webb, Gill, & Poe, 2005) believed that online distance education research needs to precede course-by-course because teaching strategies and technologies that fit in one course may not fit in another course.

In addition, the adult learner population is growing both in number and in proportion to the traditional student population (McNair, 1998; National Center for Educational Statistics, 2007). Adult learners are enrolling on campuses that offer online distance education programs (Compton, et al. 2006). However, administrators are confronted with between 40% to 80% of online students dropping out of online classes (Tyler-Smith, 2006) while at least 21% of those dropping out are pleading for richer and more engaging online learning experiences (Kim & Bonk, 2006; Schaffhauser, 2009).

This study attempted to obtain a convenience sample of approximately 250 adult learners. Su's (2006) study that surveyed online graduate learners engaging in a virtual classrooms rate of return from his online survey was 41.3%. In this study, all adult learners enrolled in two sessions of an online graduate course were asked to participate in this study.

Setting

The setting of the study is the virtual classroom on an online international campus. The campus's web-based instructional delivery model focuses on concept formation and skill development through collaborative learning. In order to meet the unique needs and modes of online learners, the campus utilizes a proprietary learning design known as the Integrated Learning Environment (ILE). The ILE presents the integration of:

1. Technology and instructor-led instruction

2. Anytime/Anywhere learning and real-time interaction, support and feedback

3. Self-directed and instructor-initiated instruction

4. Competency-based vocational and academic skill development.

The campus follows the 10-week quarter system. Each quarter consists of two five-week sessions. Students are not permitted to take over two courses at a time. Each course includes five learning units that consist of two learning events. Each learning unit contains three basic elements:

1. Presentation - Instructor-led synchronous presentation using live streaming audio. These live sessions are recorded so that students can view the instructor-led presentation at a time convenient for them. In addition, students view pre-programmed presentations using on-demand streaming video, podcast audio, or podcast video.

2. Structured Learning Support – using synchronous and asynchronous e-learning modules students investigate, discuss, and experience concepts as a group. In the group project, the students use discussion boards, chat rooms, and space on a server to upload their files for collaboration. For individual projects, students research, gather, and analyze information found in the campus online library or other credible sources.

3. Knowledge Construction - using synchronous and asynchronous discussion,

students explore course material in order to complete projects that will be assessed by the instructor based on performance, articulation, reflection, and demonstration mastery of course competencies.

Each element can be assembled in a variety of ways to support the learning event. Learning events utilize individual projects, group projects, and class discussions depending on the learning event. Flexibility of learning events constructions allows the course developer and faculty to match an effective web-based instructional strategy to match course content. Each learning event produces a product that is evaluated on an outcomes mastery model for learning assessment. Students earn points for projects and discussions which are correlated into grades. In higher education, students enrolled in degree programs learning outcome is generally measured by their grades (Hagedorn, 2005).

In the campus virtual classroom, adult learners can acquire web-based instructions via synchronous or asynchronous multimedia presentation. Adult learners are required to discuss course materials with their instructor and other learners using discussion boards. They can acquire course content by reading e-books, electronic articles, or on-demand multimedia presentations. In addition, adult learners can interact with their instructor and other learners by employing e-mail, instant messaging, text messaging, and engaging in chat rooms.

Instrument/Measures

The survey instrument selected for this study was based on the instrument used by Jennifer Percival and Bill Muirhead in their 2009 study of e-learning tools used in a hybrid and traditional course. The Percival and Muirhead (2009) study was based on Milne's 2006 study that observed that traditional classrooms are not the only form of learning space and many students view courses delivered using Internet technology as a natural and expected aspect of their lives. Percival and Muirhead's instrument was chosen because it has been used and tested as well as its relevant to this study.

This study instrument is divided into five sets of questions. The first set of questions was used to collect demographic information and to identify if the learner was enrolled on an online or blended campus. The second set of questions collected data about the type and amount e-learning devices used by adult learners to access instructional activities. These questions addressed the first hypothesis. The third, fourth, and fifth set of questions collected data about the type and amount of e-learning media used by adult learners to access online instructional activities. These questions addressed the second hypothesis. E-learning devices and media counts were used to compare the frequency and expected frequency of the counts of e-learning technologies used by adult learners enrolled on a blended campus and adult learners enrolled on an online campus. This comparison addressed the third hypothesis.

Percival and Muirhead used a 5-point Likert-type scale to count usage. Percival and Muirhead have used this survey for two years in subsequent classes and find the instrument to be reliable in determining students' engagement with e-learning modules. In this study, the survey was pilot tested using a similar sample from a previous session.

Data Collection

Data collection began after the pilot test was completed and approval had been submitted by the site administrator and Capella University. The provost officer of the online university was contacted by telephone and through e-mail in order to share the purpose and requirements of the study. A protocol for the study was submitted by the researcher to the university for approval. After approval was given, a sponsor was assigned to forward the researcher's e-mails to students.

The first e-mail announced that the E-Learning Technology Survey would be e-mailed to participants in a week. This e-mail also explained the purpose of the survey A second e-mail was sent a week later that contained the purpose of the study, how data was stored, contact information of the researcher and the Provost and Chief Academic Officer at the study's university site, as well as letting participants know that participation in the survey was voluntary. In addition, the second e-mail contained a link to a secure web-based survey that allowed participants to submit their responses anonymously. The last e-mail sent was an e-mail that reminded participants of the study. The researcher downloaded data collected from the Internet site to a password protected Excel spreadsheet then deleted all data in the Internet data base in order to be the only one with access to student data. After 7 years the researcher will destroy all data.

Snapshot surveys have been used by researchers to determine the extent of e-learning technology employed by students in learning environments (Radlick, Stefl-Mabry, & Theroux, n.d.; Browne, 1998). In this study, respondents will anonymously complete a web-based survey and submit it over the web into a password-protected online data base by clicking the submit button. The survey web site will only allow the participant to complete the survey once. In addition, respondents will be advised that participation in this study is strictly voluntary and they can skip any question on the survey that they choose not to answer.

A web-based survey was the right method for collecting this data because respondents are located in different geographical areas and time zones. In addition, respondents are using web-based technology to access their courses. Respondents should be comfortable with this form of media.

Data Analysis

Fowler (2002) believed that one purpose of a survey is to produce quantitative descriptions about an aspect of the study population. SPSS 15.0 was used to analyze demographic data. Minitab 15.0 was used to analyze quantitative data in order to compare e-learning technologies used by adult learners to access their instructor, course content, and other learners in a virtual classroom. Contingency table analysis was used to examine the differences between the categorical variables. The statistical tool used to test categorical variables for independence was the chi-square test and the chi-square goodness-of-fit test. Missing data is information that is missing in a data record (Cooper & Schindler, 2006). Records with missing data will be included in the study.

Validity and Reliability

In order to ensure analytical accuracy, a reliability test was performed on the measuring instrument prior to performing the hypotheses analysis. Cronbach's alpha for all questions except number 6 was over .70 (see Table 1). A reliability coefficient of .70 or higher is considered "acceptable" in most social research. The reliability coefficient for question 6 was .011. When data has a multidimensional structure the Cronbach's alpha is low. This indicates that some of the variables in question 6 should have been combined. The researcher believes this was the issue because handheld devices are new and evolving with similar capabilities. Therefore, each device should not have been separate but combined because of their similar capabilities to access instructors, course content, and other learners.

Table 1
Instrument Reliability Statistics

Question	α	No. of items
6	.011	6
7	.797	8
8	.864	7
9	.876	11

54

In this quantitative study, data was collected from one online university that used multiple e-learning technologies that are used at other traditional, online, and blended campuses. The participants were not coerced and were allowed to complete the survey anonymously. Anonymity is one way to ensure validity is retained (Cooper & Schindler, 2006). Swanson and Holton (2005) believed when quantitative data answers questions it claims to answer it has internal validity. If the observations can be generalized to other locations, it has external validity. The data collected in this study answered the hypotheses.

According to Cooper and Schindler (2006), the quantitative researcher attempts to control and/or manipulate the variables in experimental research. This is because it is believed that the researcher must exert substantial control over the data-gathering process in order to achieve internal validity (Swanson & Holton, 2005). This makes the results of the analytical approach generalized and not applicable in every situation (Cooper & Schindler, 2006). Despite this, the analytical approach has produced business theories, concepts, and methods (Swanson & Holton, 2005).

Limitation of this quantitative study was data was retrieved from one university that has an online campus and four blended campuses. In addition, data was only collected from adult learners who attended the same online distance education graduate course. Therefore the study may not be applicable to all campuses or distance education courses.

Ethical Considerations

The Institutional Review Board (IRB) is responsible for overseeing research involving human subjects (Fowler, 2002). The IRB is designed to protect human subjects, researchers, and its institution (p. 147). If a survey involves a level of risk to human subjects, the IRB has to formally review all procedures to make sure the human subjects are protected from damage (p. 148).

Participants were not subjected to any threats to their physical, mental, or emotional well-being. All participation in this research project was voluntary. All participants who met the standard for inclusion in the frame population had equal opportunity to participate in this research. The researcher was honest in presenting the purpose of the study to potential participants and in presenting data after the completion of the study.

All individuals have a right to privacy. Privacy ensures that validity is retained and participants are protected (Cooper & Schindler, 2006). Privacy, confidentiality, and anonymity allow participants to respond honestly during research. Participants had full disclosure on how the research would be conducted and how their information would be used in the study (Cooper & Schindler, 2006). All information from participants was protected and treated as confidential. All information will be destroyed after 7 years.

CHAPTER 4. RESULTS

Introduction

The purposes of this chapter are to present the research findings and survey results. In addition, the statistical techniques used to analyze the research hypotheses are discussed. The focus of this study is e-learning technology used by adult learners in a virtual classroom. An adult learner is defined as someone over the age of twenty-five who is employed full, part-time, or has family and community responsibilities, and is motivated to attend college (Kasworm, 2003). A virtual classroom is a course offered by a campus that allows students to interact with their instructor, course content, and other learners employing synchronous and asynchronous e-learning media (Hansen, 2001).

The survey collected data about which e-learning technologies adult learners used to access their instructor, course content, and other learners. The survey data provided information to address if there is a difference between the counts of e-learning technologies used by adult learners enrolled on a blended campus and adult learners enrolled on an online campus when accessing their instructor, course content, and other learners in the same virtual classroom. The survey also collected data about e-learning media usage of adult learners by age. Although data collected about age is not used to address the hypotheses in this study, age data is tested to determine if there is a difference in e-learning media usage by age categories.

Analysis

The sample for this study was drawn from two sessions of one graduate course offered at an online university. Blended and online adult learners enrolled in the same online graduate course were e-mailed an Internet link to the study's web-based survey by the researcher's sponsor at the online university. The survey was sent to all students enrolled in the course during two sessions; however, students twenty-four and younger were automatically excluded from completing the survey after indicating their age group. Therefore, data was collected from only adult learners, twenty-five and older enrolled in the online graduate course.

The number of surveys distributed was unknown to the researcher because this information is classified. The number of surveys completed by adult learners attending the online graduate course during two sessions was 61. Three of these surveys were rejected due to insufficient data, resulting in 58 usable surveys. In the pilot study, the survey was distributed to 50 learners enrolled in one session. It is unknown how many of these learners were adult learners (25 or older); however, the response rate was 30%. In addition, Su's (2006) study of students' engaging in online environment response rate was 41.3%.

Data was exported from the web-based survey into an Excel spreadsheet, SPSS 15.0, and Minitab 15.0. First, demographic data was analyzed using descriptive statistics to identify respondents' characteristics without testing the hypothesis. The demographic data collected but not used in performing the hypotheses analysis were age, gender, occupational status, and income level (see Appendix A). In addition, age data was collected to test statistical differences in the age of adult learners and e-learning media used by them (see Appendix B).

The results of those responding to demographic questions indicated that there were more females participating in the graduate course during the two sessions; (see Figure A3). Most participants were between the ages of 40 to 50 years old; (see Figure A1). Most respondents were professional; (see Figure A2) or earned an income between $50,000 – 75,000; (see Figure A4). Responses also indicated that more students enrolled on an online campus participated in this distance learning graduate course than those enrolled on a blended campus (see Figure A5).

Age and E-Learning Media Use

Chi-square goodness-of-fit test was used to analyze counts of e-learning media usage by age. See Appendix B. The researcher believed that distribution of usage would be uniform. The probability distribution for each e-learning media use was .0588235. The observed frequency of use was compared to the expected frequency of use in order to measure the amount by which the observed frequency distribution deviated from the expected frequency use.

In all age groups the assumption that there are no statistical differences in the e-learning media used by adult learners can not be rejected. This conclusion was drawn from chi-square goodness of fit testing and the probability value. The level of significance used to test the data was set at 0.05. *P* value was greater than .05 and the chi-square test statistic was less than the critical values of each test (see Appendix B).

E-learning media were grouped by ages and categorized into 17 categories (see Appendix C). The actual frequency and expected frequency of e-learning media counts were compared and analyzed using the chi-square test. The level of significance to test the data was set at 0.05. The total chi-square test results was 12.268. The degree of freedom was 64, which indicated a critical value of 83.675. However, one cell had an expected count of less than 1 and eight cells had an expected count less than 5 (see Table C1). This probably makes the chi-square approximation invalid. Therefore, the chi-square test was run again eliminating the text messaging category which included the cell with an expected count of less than one and five of the cells with less than five expected count (see Table C2). The total chi-square test statistic continued to be less than the critical value from the chi-square table. The *p* value was 1.000. Therefore, the assumption that there are no statistical differences in the e-learning media used by adult learners in different age groups can not be rejected.

Examination of Hypotheses

The variables used to address hypotheses were campus type, e-learning devices, and e-learning media. Chi-square goodness-of-fit test was used to analyze counts for each e-learning device and medium used by adult learners to access their instructor, course content, and other learners. Chi-square tests were used to analyze adult learners' e-learning technologies usage by campus type.

The research question driving this research is to determine if there is a difference between the counts of e-learning technologies used by adult learners enrolled on a blended campus and adult learners enrolled on an online campus when engaging their instructor, course content, and other learners in the same virtual classroom. The three research questions are:

1. What Internet devices are adult learners using to access their instructor, course content, and other learners?

2. What e-learning media are adult learners using to engage their instructor, course content, and other learners?

3. Is there a difference between the counts of e-learning technologies used by adult learners enrolled on a blended campus and adult learners enrolled on an online campus when engaging their instructor, course content, and other learners in the same virtual classroom?

What follows is an examination of these research questions' hypotheses.

Hypothesis 1

Hypothesis 1 tested for statistical differences in the number of adult learners using different types of e-learning devices to access their instructor, course content, and other learners. Adult learners used personal computers, laptops, and handheld mobile devices to access their instructor, course content, and other learners. The

61

researcher believed that distribution of usage would be uniform (.333333) for adult

learners using these e-learning devices to access their instructor, course content, or

other learners. The observed frequency of use was compared to the expected

frequency of use in order to measure the amount by which the observed frequency

deviated from the expected frequency (see Table 2).

Table 2

E-Learning Devices Used to Access Instructor, Course Content, or Other Learners

E-Learning Device	f	x^2
Personal computer	39	0.4571
Laptop	54	10.3143
Handheld mobile	12	15.1143
Total	105	25.8857

Note. $f_e = 35$. $\alpha = 0.05$. $*p = 0.000$.

There were three categories of e-learning devices adult learners used to access

their instructor, course content, or other learners. The number of degrees of freedom

is 2. Two degrees of freedom in the chi-square table equates to a critical value of

5.99. Since test statistic 25.8857 is greater than the critical value from the chi-square

table, the null hypothesis is rejected. In addition, the level of significance to test the

data was set at 0.05. *P*-value for frequency counts was 0.000 which is less than 0.05.

This analysis indicated the null hypothesis can be rejected. There is a statistical

difference in the number of adult learners using different types of Internet devices to

access their instructor, course content, and other learners.

In this study, adult learners use personal computers, laptops, and handheld

mobile devices in varying degrees. Laptops were used more than expected and handheld devices were used less than expected. Therefore, the null hypothesis is rejected and the alternative hypothesis is accepted.

Hypothesis 2

Hypothesis 2 tested for statistical differences in the number of adult learners using different types of e-learning media to access their instructor, course content, and other learners. Counts of e-learning media usage were examined by instructor, course content, and other learners and analyzed using the chi-square goodness-of-fit test for Observed Counts. The e-learning media used by adult learners to access their instructor were categorized into eight specific categories (see Table 3). The researcher believed that distribution of usage would be uniform.

E-learning media use to access instructors. The probability distribution for the eight e-learning media categorize used by adult learners to access their instructor was .0.125. The actual number of observations was totaled for each e-learning media category. The observed frequency of use was compared to the expected frequency of use (36.125) in order to measure the amount by which the observed frequency deviated from the expected frequency.

The level of significance to test the data was set at 0.05. The number of degrees of freedom is 7. Seven degrees of freedom in the chi-square table equates to a critical value of 14.067. Since test statistic 58.4879 is greater than the critical value from the chi-square table, the null hypothesis is rejected. In addition, the p-value was 0.000 which is less than 0.05 indicating that the null hypothesis can be rejected.

63

Therefore, there is a significant difference in e-learning media used by adult learners to access their instructor.

Table 3
E-Learning Media Used to Access Instructor

E-learning media	f	x^2
Live Web Conference	42	0.9554
Recorded Web Conference	49	4.5887
Instant Messaging	13	14.8032
E-Mails	44	1.7167
Texting	5	26.8170
Classroom DB	53	7.8828
Group DB	40	0.4157
Posting Files	43	1.3084
Total	289	58.4879

Note. f_e = 36.125. α = 0.05. *p = 0.000.

E-learning media usage to access other learners. The e-learning media used by adult learners to access other learners were categorized by specific media selected (see Table 4). The probability distribution for e-learning media used by adult learners to access other learners was .142857. The observed frequency of usage was compared to the expected frequency of usage in order to measure the amount by which the observed frequency deviated from the expected frequency use (35.8571)

The level of significance to test the data was set at 0.05. The number of degrees of freedom is 6 . Six degrees of freedom in the chi-square table equates to a critical value of 12.592. Since test statistic 50.1673 is greater than the critical value from the chi-square table 12.592, the null hypothesis is rejected. In addition, the *P*-value was 0.000 which is less than 0.05. This value indicates that the null hypothesis should be rejected and the alternative hypotheses accepted. There is a statistical difference in

64

the number of adult learners using different types of e-learning media to access other

learners.

Table 4
E-Learning Media Used to Access Other Learners

E-learning media	f	x^2
Live Web Conferencing	42	1.0524
Instant Messaging	26	2.7097
E-Mails	49	4.8173
Classroom DB	51	6.3950
Group DB	50	5.5783
Text Messaging	4	28.3034
Posting Files	29	1.3113
Total	251	50.1673

Note. $f_e = 35.8571$. $\alpha = 0.05$. *$p = 0.000$.

E-learning media usage to access course content. Since only asynchronous

media was used to access course content in this study, counts of e-learning media

usage were categorized by each asynchronous media and analyzed using the chi-

square goodness-of-it est for observed counts (see Table 5.). The probability

distribution for e-learning device media was 0.1. The observed frequency of use was

compared to the expected frequency of use (49.9) in order to measure the amount by

which the observed frequency distribution deviated from the expected frequency use.

The level of significance to test the data was set at 0.05. The number of degrees

of freedom is 9. Nine degrees of freedom in the chi-square table equates to a critical

value of 16.919. Since the chi-square test statistic 4.6725 is less than the critical value

from the chi-square table, this part of the null hypothesis can not be rejected. The P-

value was 0.866 and is greater than 0.05. This indicates that the null hypothesis should not be rejected. There is no statistical difference in the number of adult

learners using different types of e-learning media to access their course content.

Table 5
E-Learning Media Used to Access Course Content

E-learning media	f	x^2
Multimedia Presentation	45	0.48116
Multimedia Text	52	0.08838
Multimedia Questions	45	0.48116
Multimedia Activity	41	1.58737
Course Resources	49	0.01623
Announcements	57	1.01022
Internet Articles	55	0.52124
Syllabus	52	0.08838
Instructor Comments	54	0.33687
Others Comments	49	0.01623
Total	499	4.62725

Note. $f_e = 49.9$. $\alpha = 0.05$. $p = 0.866$.

Since chi-square test statistics of e-learning media used by adult learners to

access their instructor and other learners was greater than their critical value and the *p*

value was less than 0.05, the null hypothesis was rejected and the alternative

hypothesis is accepted. There is a statistical difference in the number of adult learners

using different types of e learning media to access their instructor and other learners.

However, the chi-square test statistics of e-learning media used by adult learners to

access their course content was less than the critical value. In addition, the p value

was greater than 0.05. Therefore, the null hypothesis cannot be rejected. There is no

statistical difference in the number of adult learners using different types of e-

learning media to access their course content.

Hypothesis 3

Hypothesis 3 tested for statistical differences in the number of adult learners enrolled on blended campuses and adult learners enrolled on an online campus using different types of e-learning technologies to access their instructor, course content, and other learners. Counts of e-learning technology use were grouped by campus type - online and blended. The e-learning technologies used by adult learners to access their instructor, course content, and other learners were tested by devices and media used. Data was analyzed using the chi-square test (see Tables 6, 7, 8, and 9).

E-learning device usage by campus type. E-learning devices were grouped by personal computers and mobile devices. The expected count for handheld mobile devices was less than five. Therefore, handheld mobile devices and laptops were grouped together. The rational for this grouping is because laptops are also mobile devices. The actual frequency and expected frequency were compared by campus type. Adult learners' use of e-learning devices to access their instructor, course content, and other learners were analyzed using the chi-square test (see Table 6).

The level of significance to test the data was set at 0.05. The degree of freedom was 1 which indicated a critical value of 3.841. The chi-square test result was 0.029 for adult learners using e-learning devices to access their instructor. Since the chi-square test value is less than the critical value, the null hypothesis cannot be rejected. In addition, the p value of 0.866 is greater than 0.05 which indicates that the null hypothesis should not be rejected. Therefore, there is no statistical difference in the

67

number of adult learners enrolled on blended campuses and adult learners enrolled on an online campus using different types of e-learning devices to access their instructor, course content, and other learners.

Table 6

Comparative E-Learning Device Use by Campus Type

| E-learning Device | Campus Type | | Total X^2 |
	Online	Blended	
Personal Computer			
f	32.000	7.000	
f_e	32.310	6.690	
X^2	0.003	0.015	0.018
Mobile			
f	55.000	11.000	
f_e	54.690	11.310	
X^2	0.002	0.009	0.011
Total X^2			0.029

Note. $\alpha = 0.05$. $p = 0.866$.

E-learning media use by campus type to access instructors. E-learning media were grouped by campus type and categorized into eight categories to compare and analyze the actual and expected frequency use of media used to access instructors (see Table 7). The level of significance to test the data was set at 0.05. The overall chi-square test results was 6.943. The degree of freedom was 7 which indicated a critical value of 14.067. Since the chi-square test value is less than the critical value, the null hypothesis cannot be rejected. In addition, the *p*-value was 0.435. Since the *p*-value is greater than 0.05 the null hypotheses cannot be rejected for e-learning media used by adult learners to access the instructor. There are no statistical differences in the number of adult learners enrolled on blended campuses and adult learners enrolled on an online campus using different types of e-learning media to

68

access their instructor.

Table 7

Comparative E-Learning Media Use by Campus Type to Access Instructor

E-learning Device	Campus Type		Total X^2
	Online	Blended	
Live Web Conference			
f	59.000	14.000	
f_e	60.020	12.980	
X^2	0.017	0.081	0.098
Recorded Web Conference			
f	73.000	10.000	
f_e	68.240	14.760	
X^2	0.331	1.533	1.864
Instant Messaging			
f	16.000	5.000	
f_e	17.270	3.730	
X^2	0.093	0.430	0.523
E-mails			
f	53.000	15.000	
f_e	55.910	12.090	
X^2	0.152	0.701	0.853
Group Discussion Board			
f	75.000	16.000	
fe	74.820	16.180	
$X2$	0.000	0.002	0.002
Class Discussion Board			
f	95.000	19.000	
f_e	93.730	20.270	
X^2	0.017	0.079	0.096
Texting *Continued*			
f	6.000	4.000	
f_e	8.220	1.780	
X^2	0.601	2.778	3.379
Postings Files			
f	67.000	13.000	
f_e	65.780	14.220	
X^2	0.023	0.105	0.128
Total X^2			6.943

Note. $\alpha = 0.05$. $p = 0.435$.

E-learning media use by campus type to access other learners. E-learning

media were grouped by campus type and categorized into seven specific categories (see Table 8). The actual frequency and expected frequency were compared and

analyzed using the chi-square test for each e-learning media used to access other

learners. The level of significance to test the data was set at 0.05. The overall chi-

square test results was 11.074. The degree of freedom was 6 which indicated a critical

value of 12.592. Since the chi-square test value is less than the critical value, the null

hypothesis is not rejected. P-value was 0.086. Since the p-value is greater than 0.05

the null hypotheses cannot be rejected for e-learning media used adult learners to

access other learners. There are no statistical differences in the number of adult

learners enrolled on blended campuses and adult learners enrolled on an online

campus using different types of e-learning media to access other learners.

Table 8

Comparative E-Learning Media Use by Campus Type to Access Other Learners

E-learning Device	Campus Type		Total X^2
	Online	Blended	
Live Web Conference			
f	66.000	9.000	
f_e	61.970	13.030	
X^2	0.262	1.247	1.509
InstantMessaging			
f	42.000	7.000	
f_e	40.490	8.510	
X^2	0.057	0.269	0.326
Emails			
f	70.000	19.000	
f_e	73.540	15.460	
X^2	0.170	0.809	0.979
Group Discussion Board			
f	82.000	15.000	
f_e	80.150	16.850	
X^2	0.043	0.204	0.247
Class Discussion Board			
f	100.000	16.000	
f_e	95.850	20.150	
X^2	0.180	0.856	1.036

| E-learning Device | Campus Type | | Total X^2 |
	Online	Blended	
Texting			
f	7.000	4.000	
f_e	9.090	1.910	
X^2	0.480	2.283	2.763
Postings Files			
f	42.000	16.000	
f_e	47.920	10.080	
X^2	0.732	3.482	4.214
Total X^2			11.074

Note. $\alpha = 0.05$. $p = 0.086$.

E-learning media use by campus type to access course content. E-learning

media were grouped by campus type and categorized into ten specific categories (see

Table 9). The actual frequency and expected frequency were compared and analyzed

using the chi-square test for each e-learning media used to access course content. The

level of significance to test the data was set at 0.05. The total chi-square test results

for each asynchronous media used to access course content was 4.595. The degree of

freedom was 9 which indicated a critical value of 16.919. Since the chi-square test

value is less than the critical value, the null hypothesis cannot be rejected. *P*-value

was 0.868. Since the p-value is greater than 0.05 the null hypotheses cannot be

rejected for e-learning media used by adult learners to access course content. There

are no statistical differences in the number of adult learners enrolled on blended

campuses and adult learners enrolled on an online campus using different types of e-

learning media to access course content.

Table 9

Comparative E-Learning Media Use by Campus Type to Access Course Content

E-learning Device	Campus Type		Total X^2
	Online	Blended	
Multimedia Presentation			
f	71.000	12.000	
f_e	70.170	12.830	
X^2	0.010	0.054	0.064
Multimedia Text			
f	98.000	12.000	
f_e	92.990	17.010	
X^2	0.269	1.474	1.743
Multimedia Questions			
f	75.000	10.000	
f_e	71.860	13.140	
X^2	0.137	0.751	0.888
Multimedi: *Continued*			
f	70.000	12.000	
f_e	69.320	12.680	
X^2	0.007	0.036	0.043
Course Material			
f	85.000	15.000	
f_e	84.540	15.460	
X^2	0.030	0.014	0.017
Announcements			
f	97.000	23.000	
f_e	101.450	18.550	
X^2	0.195	1.067	1.262
Internet Articles			
f	117.000	24.000	
f_e	119.200	21.800	
X^2	0.041	0.222	0.263
Syllabus			
f	69.000	14.000	
f_e	70.170	12.830	
X^2	0.019	0.106	0.125
Instructor Comments			
f	92.000	18.000	
f_e	92.990	17.010	
X^2	0.011	0.058	0.069
Learners' Comments			
f	90.000	18.000	
f_e	91.300	16.700	
X^2	0.019	0.102	0.121
Total X^2			4.595

Note. α = 0.05. *p* = 0.868.

Since the *p* value of e-learning media and devices used by adult learners on an online and blended campuses to access their instructor, course content, and other learners was greater than 0.05 and all chi-square test values are less than their critical values, the null hypothesis cannot be rejected. There are no statistical differences in the number of adult learners enrolled on a blended campus and adult learners enrolled on an online campus using different types of e-learning technologies to access their instructor, course content, and other learners.

Summary

There was a significant difference in the number of adult learners using different types of Internet devices to access their instructor, course content, and other learners. There was a statistical difference in the number of adult learners using different types of e-learning media to access their instructor and other learners. There was no significant difference in the number of adult learners using different types of e-learning media to access their course content. There were no significant differences in the number of adult learners enrolled on blended campuses and adult learners enrolled on an online campus using different types of e-learning technologies to access their instructor, course content, and other learners. Chapter 5 discusses the results of the research and implications for future research.

CHAPTER 5. DISCUSSION, IMPLICATION, RECOMMENDATION

Introduction

The purpose of this study was to investigate e-learning technologies used by adult learners enrolled on blended and online campuses to access their instructor, course content, and other learners in a virtual classroom. In addition, e-learning technologies used by students on blended campuses were compared to e-learning technologies used by students on an online campus to determine if these two populations used e-learning technologies differently. This chapter discusses the results and recommendations based on analysis of research data collected during the study. In addition, the limitation of the study and implications for future research are provided.

Discussion

The research question driving this research was to determine if there is a difference between the counts of e-learning technologies used by adult learners enrolled on a blended campus and adult learners enrolled on an online campus when accessing their instructor, course content, and other learners in the same virtual classroom. The three research questions were:

1. What Internet devices are adult learners using to access their instructor, course content, and other learners?

2. What e-learning media are adult learners using to engage their instructor,

74

course content, and other learners?

3. Is there a difference between the counts of e-learning technologies used by adult learners enrolled on a blended campus and adult learners enrolled on an online campus when engaging their instructor, course content, and other learners in the same virtual classroom?

The convergence of competition, cost, technology, and new consumer demands have suggested that there are different rules for engaging students in a historically placid environment that has derived its strength from tradition rather than transition (Beaudoin, 2002). Confusion increases as higher education leaders explore dozens of new e-learning technologies to engage learners (Kim & Bonk, 2006). In a learner-centered world, student selection of e-learning technologies may better predict how to engage students in an online distance education course (Kim & Bonk, 2006; Percival & Muirhead, 2009; Su, 2006). In addition, Yu (1998) believed that counting the use of e-learning technologies in a virtual classroom can reflect user engagement.

During online courses, learners use synchronous and asynchronous online instructional activities to engage their instructor, course content, and other learners (Carter, 2008; Hwong, 2003; Su, 2006; Zhang, 2003). Learners engage instructors and other learners in online distance education courses by posting on discussion boards, attending faculty live chat sessions, instant messaging their instructor and other learners, viewing faculty recorded chat sessions, viewing faculty and other learner comments, reading announcement postings, and e-mailing their instructor and

75

other learners (Dron, 2007). In addition, students receive online instruction using on-demand streaming media (Zhang, 2003).

Beaudoin (2002) pointed out that online distance education should be central to an educational institution's strategic plan for success in the new global marketplace. Before deciding to implement new processes to meet an objective, leaders of online organizations must consider the mission of the organization (Levitt & March, 1988) and identify the organization's core competencies (Nevis, DiBella, & Gould, 1995). One core competency of an online campus is their use of e-learning technologies.

An online campus offers students the ability to attend a course in a virtual classroom (Singh, O'Donoghue, & Betts, 2002). A blended campus provides courses in their degree program that can be taken in virtual classrooms, traditional classrooms, or by means of both online and traditional instructions (Webb, Gill, & Poe, 2005). A virtual classroom is one section of multiple sections of a course offered during a session by a campus that allows students to interact with their instructor, course content, and other learners employing synchronous and asynchronous e-learning media (Hansen, 2001).

This study used quantitative data to analyze adult learners' use of e-learning technologies. Percival and Muirhead (2009) survey instrument was used to collect data about e-learning technologies used by students enrolled in a hybrid and a traditional course. Percival and Muirhead (2009) survey was modified and used in this study to collect e-learning technologies used by adult learners enrolled in a

76

blended and online course. The study instrument was divided into five sets of questions. The first set of questions was used to identify the demographic characteristics of the learners and to ensure that they were twenty-five years or older. The second set of questions collected data about the type and counts e-learning devices used by adult learners to access their instructor, course content, and other learners. The third, fourth, and fifth set of questions collected data about the type and counts of e-learning media used by adult learners to access their instructor, course content, and other learners. The reliability of one of the questions in the survey instrument is in question. This may be resolved by increasing the sample size and grouping similar handheld devices into one category. For example, personal computers and laptops were not separated into smaller categories. Therefore, mobile handheld devices could have been group together.

In addition, a critical limitation for interpreting the results was due to the small sample size. The sample size should be large enough to give a good idea of the behavior of the population. Since the population size was confidential, it was not clear if the amount of information collected was adequate. The larger the sample you take of the population the closer the results of the sample will be to the population (Pelosi & Sandifer, 2002).

The results of this study indicated that most respondents participating in this online graduate course were between the ages of 40 to 50 years old (see Figure A1). Most were professional (see Figure A2). More females participated in the online

77

graduate course during the two sessions (see Figure A3). Most respondents earned an income between $50,000 – 75,000 (see Figure A4). Most respondents were enrolled on the online campus; see Figure A5. In all age groups (over 25, 25 – 30, 30 -40, 40 – 50, and over 50), there was not a significant difference in the e-learning media used by adult learners to access their instructor, course content, and other learners (see Appendix F). In addition, there was no statistical differences in the e-learning media used by adult learners within different age groups (see Appendix C).

There was a significant difference in the number of adult learners using different types of Internet devices to access their instructor, course content, and other learners. Laptops were used the most by adult learners in this study to access their instructor, course content, and other learners (see Tables 2). Adult learners also used personal computers. Handheld mobile devices were used the least by adult learners.

There was a statistical difference in the number of adult learners using different types of e-learning media to access their instructor and other learners. Adult learners access their instructor using the classroom discussion board more often than any other media (see Table 3). However, posting on the classroom discussion board was required. Adult learners were not required to use recorded chat sessions and this was the second highest method used to access their instructor. Adult learners accessed other learners the most using the discussion boards and e-mails (see Table 4). The media used the least by adult learners to access their instructor or other learners was text messaging. There was no significant difference in the number of adult learners using different types of e-learning media to access their course content (see Table 5). There were no significant differences in the number of adult learners enrolled on a blended campus and adult learners enrolled on an online campus using different types of e-learning technologies to access their instructor, course content, and other learners (see Tables 6, 7, 8, and 9).

The limitation of this quantitative study is data was retrieved from one university that has an online campus and four blended campuses. In addition, data was only collected from adult learners who had taken one online graduate course at this university. Therefore, the study may not be applicable to all campuses or online distance education courses.

Implications for Future Research

Several researchers believe that online distance education research needs to precede course-by-course because teaching strategies and technologies that fit in one course may not fit in another course (Carter, 2008; Charlson, 2006; Moore & Kearsley, 2005; Percival & Muirhead, 2009; Su, 2006; Webb, Gill, & Poe, 2005). The online campus in this study provided an online graduate distance education course to students enrolled on their blended and online campuses in the same virtual classrooms. Although theories have been developed about e-learning technologies used in online distance education (Ally, 2008; Bates, 2001; Percival & Muirhead, 2009; Tapscott & Williams, 2008; & Zhang, 2003), there was no research about adult learners enrolled on two different campuses (online and blended) interacting in the same virtual classroom. In this study, adult learners enrolled on blended and online campuses did not use e-learning technologies in different degrees. This study adds to the previous mentioned researchers' body of knowledge by expanding e-learning technology usage by adult learners on two campus types accessing their instructor, course content, and other learners in one online distance education environment.

The adult learner population is growing (National Center for Educational Statistics, 2007) and they are enrolling in distance education courses hoping they will be able to fit acquiring a degree into their busy lives (Kasworm, 2003). However, between 40% to 80% drop out of online classes (Tyler-Smith, 2006) and 21% are pleading for a more engaging online experience (Kim & Bonk, 2006; Schaffhauser, 2009). Confusion increases as higher education leaders explore dozens of new e-learning technologies to engage learners (Kim & Bonk, 2006). This study also provided online campus administrators with comparative insights on the e-learning technologies used by adult learners enrolled on two different campuses (online and blended) sharing the same virtual classroom. In a learner-centered world, student selection of e-learning technologies may better predict how to engage students in an online distance education course (Kim & Bonk, 2006; Percival & Muirhead, 2009; Su, 2006). In this study, adult learners used laptops the most and handheld mobile devices the least to access their instructor, course content, and other learners.

Future research should be expanded to include all learners enrolled on blended and online campuses but participating in the same virtual classroom. Increasing the sample size may improve reliability of the instrument and give campus administrators a better perspective of all learners enrolled in the online course. In addition, future research should investigate learners' use of e-learning technologies course by course at online universities because e-learning technologies used in one online course may not fit in another online course (Carter, 2008; Charlson, 2006; Moore & Kearsley, 2005; Percival & Muirhead, 2009; Su, 2006; Webb, Gill, & Poe, 2005).

Recommendations

Because of confidentiality issues, it was not clear how many learners were enrolled in the online graduate course over the two sessions. Therefore, there may not have been enough learners in the two sessions to expand the sample size if all learners were included. If this was the case, the study should be expanded over more sessions. However, this may be impractical because technology is changing rapidly. Therefore, the best research may result in the researcher being able to access confidential information about the make-up of learners enrolled in the online distance education course. Therefore, one recommendation is that research be conducted course by course; however, the researcher should be allowed access to confidential information.

In addition, this researcher believes that the instrument used to collect data can be improved. The question that collected data about device use by adult learners needs to be modified. Handheld mobile devices should be grouped together. Personal computers and laptops were grouped together; therefore, handheld mobile devices should have been grouped together.

For the graduate course used in this study, it may not be necessary to provide course information in a format for students to access the information on handheld mobile devices at this time. This recommendation would be based on the organization's four strategic perspectives. These four strategic perspectives are; strategy as rational thought, strategy as revolution, strategy as resource allocation and accumulation, and strategy in technology leadership (Thompson, Strickland, & Gamble, 2005).

Strategy as rational thought perspective posits that organizations use their mission statement (Pearce & Robinson, 2003) and values (Thompson, et al., 2005) to determine which choices their company should select. Strategy as revolution perspective proposes that companies that manage their innovations will have a strategic advantage (Christensen, 1997). Strategy as resource allocation and accumulation suggests that appraising a company's resource strengths and weaknesses, as well as its external opportunities and threats indicates the physical condition of a company (Thompson, et al., 2005). Pearce and Robinson (2003) believed that strategy as technology leadership submits that a company must decide whether they are going to lead or follow with their use of technology. A company that decides to be first must be aware that their costs will be higher than competitors implementing the technology after them (Pearson & Robinson, 2003). This is because the cost to implement older technology is less expensive and competitors can learn from their mistakes. However, if the organization offers the learner what they want, they can earn customer loyalty (Thompson, et al., 2005).

Conclusion

This study has contributed to several researchers' investigations in e-learning technologies used in online distance education courses (Ally, 2008; Bates, 2001; Percival & Muirhead, 2009; Tapscott & Williams, 2008; & Zhang, 2003). This study investigated e-learning technologies used by adult learners enrolled on blended and online campuses to access their instructor, course content, and other learners in the same virtual classroom. In addition, e-learning technologies used by learners on blended campuses were compared to e-learning technologies used by students on an online campus to determine if these two populations used e-learning technologies differently.

Internet capabilities continue to evolve. Individuals are transitioning from dial-up Internet access to obtaining fiber optics Internet services for their homes. Communities are providing free high speed Internet access. Hotels, restaurants, bookstores, and cafés are promoting their free high speed Internet services to their customers. Wireless Internet cards are being offered by cellular telephone companies and automobile manufacturers are including Internet technology in their automobiles. Mobile devices, such as laptops and net books, are being used by facilitators and learners to participate in online e-learning events at a place convenient for them.

In this study, there was a significant difference in the number of adult learners using different types of Internet devices to access their instructor, course content, and other learners. Laptops were used the most by adult learners, some adult learners used personal computers, and the least used Internet devices were devices that provided access to the Internet that could be held in the palm of the learner's hand. This implies that the devices being used by adult learners to access their instructor, course content, and other learners are evolving from the stationary personal computers to handheld mobile devices. In 1989, learners only used personal computers (Moore & Kearsley, 2005). As laptops became sleeker with faster processing units in the 1990's, learners began using laptops. Currently, traditional colleges are requiring students to purchase laptops.

Some computer manufacturers are producing netbooks which are Internet mobile devices that are smaller than laptops. Also, computer and cellular telephone manufacturers are producing Internet devices that can be held in the palm of a user's hand. One of the issues with Internet devices that can be held in the palm of a user's hand is that the screen is smaller than other mobile devices. However, some manufacturers who produce these smaller handheld Internet mobile devices are making their device screens larger and increasing the speed in which Internet information is accessed on the device. This evolution in handheld mobile technology may increase the number of adult learners using handheld mobile devices that are smaller than laptops.

There is a statistical difference in the number of adult learners using different types of e-learning media to access their instructor and other learners. Adult learners accessed their instructor and other learners the most using discussion boards. However, learners were required to post on discussion boards. The second most used media were recorded video-conferences led by instructors. Adult learners were not required to access these forums; but these recorded video-conferences were accessed more than previously recorded multimedia presentations. This implies that adult learners may prefer listening to their instructor and other learners engaged in discussion about the course material rather than listening to a general multimedia presentation recorded by the course developer. If this is the case, campus leaders and course developers should implement in their course recorded video-conferences that include the instructor and other learners engaging about course materials.

There was no significant difference in the number of adult learners using different types of e-learning media to access their course content. Adult learners in this study preferred accessing course content by viewing the Announcement area as well as clicking on links that directed them to course materials on the Internet. This implies that learners accessed course information via the Internet only. As technology change, colleges implement these technologies into their courses (Adams, 2006). For this graduate course, paper-based text has been replaced by Internet-based text.

In addition, this study provided online campus administrators with

85

comparative insights on the e-learning technologies used by adult learners enrolled on two different campuses (online and blended) participating in an online graduate course during two sessions. There were no significant differences in the number of adult learners enrolled on a blended campus and adult learners enrolled on an online campus using different types of e-learning technologies to access their instructor, course content, and other learners. Several researchers believe that online distance education research needs to precede course-by-course because teaching strategies and technologies that fit in one course may not fit in another course (Carter, 2008; Charlson, 2006; Moore & Kearsley, 2005; Percival & Muirhead, 2009; Su, 2006; Webb, Gill, & Poe, 2005). This implies that universities and colleges offering blended and online degree programs can enroll their students in the same distance education course and address the Internet technology needs of adult learners enrolled on either of their campuses. However, the Internet technology used by adult learners maybe different based on the course. University leaders are responsible for maintaining consistency in the outcome of courses delivered to students using distance education (Paul, 1990). Campus leaders should ensure research is conducted to ensure that students enrolled on different campus types engaging in the same e-learning environment are using the same devices and media to access their instructor, course content, and other learners. Then use this information to determine e-learning technologies that should be included and excluded in each course.

Summary

In a learner-centered world, student selection of e-learning technologies may better predict how to engage students in an online distance education course (Kim & Bonk, 2006; Percival & Muirhead, 2009; Su, 2006). In this study, adult learners enrolled on a blended campus and adult learners enrolled on an online campus used laptops the most. This implies that learners are using mobile devices to access their instructor, course content, and other learners.

Internet technology is evolving. Internet devices are getting smaller and some learners have begun using these devices to access their instructor, course content, and other learners. In this study, there were not a significant number of learners using mobile handheld devices that could be held in the palm of the learners' hands. For this course, campus leaders should determine if they should include course information in a format that can be accessed only by these devices. This decision would be based on the cost of providing information in a different format for these devices and if the educational institution wants to be first, last, or somewhere in the middle when implementing new Internet technology in their e-learning environment.

Adult learners enrolled on an online campus and adult learners enrolled on blended campuses did not show any significant differences in the type of e-learning technologies they used to access their instructor, course content, and other learners while engaging in the same distance education class. Since the adult learner population is growing faster than the traditional student population (National Center for Educational Statistics, 2007) and online distance education research needs to precede course-by-course (Carter, 2008; Charlson, 2006; Moore & Kearsley, 2005; Percival & Muirhead, 2009; Su, 2006; Webb, Gill, & Poe, 2005) campus leaders at the university where the study was conducted should research each course's Internet technology use by adult learners to ensure that students enrolled on different campus types are using the same devices and media to access their instructor, course content, and other learners. Then decide which e-learning technology should be implemented in each course.

REFERENCES

Ally, M. (2008). Foundation of educational theory for online learning. In T. Anderson, *The theory and practice of online learning*. (pp. 16 - 44). Canada: AU Press, Athabasca University Press.

Adams, J. (2006). The part played by instructional media in distance education. *Studies in Media & Information Literacy Education, 6*(2), 1-6.

Barritt, M. D. (1998). *Extending educational communication: The experience of distance learning via a distributive environment for collaboration and learning* (Doctoral dissertation, University of Michigan, AAT 9825166)

Bates, A. W. (2005). *Technology, e-learning, and distance education*. London: RoutledgeFalmer.

Bates, T. (2001). National strategies for e-learning in post-secondary education and training. Retrieved October 1, 2008, from United Nations Educational, Scientific and Cultural Organization Web site: http://unesdoc.unesco.org/images/0012/001262/126230e.pdf

Beaudoin, M. F. (2002). Distance education leadership: An essential role for the new century. *Journal of Leadership Studies, 8*(3), 131-145.

Berg, G. A. (2005). Reform higher education with capitalism? *Change 37*(3), 28-34.

Browne, M. (1998). Visualizing web usage: Using data visualization to improve web site performance. *(Thesis, University of Tennessee, Knoxville)*

Capron, H. L. (1990). *Computers: Tools for an information age*. New York: The Benjamin/Cummings.

Carter, C. (2008). *The panhellenic project: Assessing learning engagement using Web 2.0 technologies*. (Dissertation, Pepperdine University, UMI 3330961)

Christensen, C. M. (1997). *The innovator's dilemma: When new technologies cause great firms to fail*. Boston: Harvard Business School Press.

Charlson, J. K. (2006). *Differences between online and traditional methods: Performance and satisfaction in an interior design course*. (Dissertation, Colorado State University, UMI 3233329)

Compton, J. I., Cox, E., & Laanan, F. S. (2006). *Understanding students in transition* [electronic version]. Retrieved August 20, 2008, from Web site: www.interscience.wiley.com

Cooper, C. R., & Schindler, P. S. (2006). *Business research methods* (9th ed.). Boston: McGraw-Hill Irwin.

Dess, G., & Picken, J. (2000). Changing roles: Leadership for the 21st century. *Organizational Dynamics, 28*(3), 18–34.

Dewey, J. (1910). *How we think.* Lexington, MA: D.C. Heath.

Devry University. (2009). Flexibility built around you. Retrieved April 25, 2009, from DeVry University Web site: http://www.devry.edu/

Dron, J. (2007). *Control and Constraint in E-Learning: Choosing When to Choose.* Hershey, PA: Information Science Pub.

Eisenbach, R., Golich, V., & Curry, R. (1998). Classroom assessment across the disciplines. *New Direction for Teaching and Learning, 75,* 59-66.

Flint, T. A. (2001, Winter). Principles of effectiveness for serving adult learners in higher education. *The Catalyst, 6,* 3.

Fowler, F. J., Jr. (2002). *Survey research methods, applied social research methods series.* Thousand Oaks, CA: Sage.

Garrison, D. R., & Anderson, T. (2003). *E-learning in the 21st century: A framework for research and practice.* New York: RoutledgeFalmer.

Hagedorn, L. S. (2005). Square pegs, adult students and their "fit" in postsecondary institutions. *Change, 37*(1), 22-29.

Hansen, B. (2001, December 7). Distance learning. *CQ Researcher, 11, 993-1016.* Retrieved March 28, 2009, from CQ Researcher Online, http://library.cqpress.com/cqresearcher/cqresrre2001120700

Harriman, G. (2004). E-learning. *E-Learning Resources.* Retrieved January 14, 2009, from http://www.grayharriman.com/e-learning.htm#6

HCC. (2006). Definition of hybrid courses. Retrieved April 25, 2009, from Highline Community College Web site: http://flightline.highline.edu/distlearn/hybrid.defn.htm#footnote

Hwong W. (2003). Internet learning: An assessment of students' Internet usage in one college in Taiwan. (*Dissertation, Spalding University, 2003*). UMI 3077707.

Kasworm, C. (2003). Setting the stage: Adults in higher education. *New Directions for Student Services, 102,* 3-10.

Kim, K., & Bonk, C. (2006). The future of online teaching and learning in higher education: The survey says .... *Education Quarterly 4,* 22 – 30.

Knowles, M. S., Holton III, E. F., & Swanson, R. A. (2005). *The Adult Learner* (6th ed.). Burlington, MA: Elsevier.

Kotter, J. P. (1996). *Leading change.* Boston: Harvard Business School Press.

Kreitzer, D. (1999). *University formal and non-formal distance education programs.* (Dissertation Ball State University, UMI 9950365)

Lester, R. K. & Piore, M. J. (2004). *Innovation: The missing dimension.* MA: Havard University

Press.

Levitt, B., & March, J. G. (1988). Organizational learning. *Annual Review of Sociology, 14*, 319-340.

Lindeman, E. (1989). *The meaning of adult education*. New York: New Republic.

McNair, S. (1998). The invisible majority: Adult learning in English higher education. *Higher Education Quarterly 52*(2), 162-178.

Meyer, M. L. (2002). Effective teaching techniques and practices in an Internet-based distance education environment (*Dissertation, California State University, Fresno, 2002*). UMI 3062341.

Moore, M., & Kearsley, G. (2005). *Distance education: A systems view*. (2nd ed.). Belmont, CA: Wadsworth.

National Center for Education Statistics. (2007). *Digest of education statistics: 2007* [electronic version]. Retrieved August 14, 2008, from http://nces.ed.gov/pubsearch/pubsinfo.asp?pubid=2007166

Nevis, E. C., Dibella, A. J., & Gould, J. M. (1995). Understanding organizations as learning systems. *Sloan Management Review, 36*, 73-85.

North Carolina State University. (n.d.). *Distance education: Learning beyond the classroom*. Retrieved December 6, 2008, from http://www.ncsu.edu/academics/distance-education/index.php

Palloff, R.M., & Pratt, K. *The virtual student: A profile and guide to working with online learners*, Jossey-Bass, 2003.

Paul, J. E. (1990). The effect of delivery systems on selected educational outcomes among nontraditional students in an undergraduate business administration degree program *(Dissertation, University of Wisconsin-Madison, 1990)*. UMI 9024778.

Paulus, T. M. (2003). Collaboration and the social construction of knowledge in an online learning environment. *(Dissertation, Indiana University, 2003)*. UMI 3119850.

Pearce, J.A., & Robinson, R. B. (2003). *Formulation, implementation, and control of competitive strategy*. New York: McGraw-Hill.

Percival, J., & Muirhead, B. (2009). Prioritizing the implementation of e-learning tools to enhance the post-secondary learning environment. *Journal of Distance Education, 23*(1), 89 -106.

Porter, M. E. (1998). *Competitive strategy: Techniques for analyzing industries and competitors*. New York: The Free Press.

Radlick, M. S., Stefl-Mabry, J., & Theroux, P. J. (n.d). Multiple views: Measuring computer use in school and outside comparing self-reported and actual usage data. *Institute for Research on Learning Technology Visions, Inc*.

Roberson, D. N. (2004). The nature of self-directed learning in older rural adults. *Ageing International, 29*(2),199-218.

Robinson, S. V. (2005). *Technology in schools: A descriptive study of computer usage in a school and its effect on bridging the digital divide.* (Dissertation, Pepperdine University, UMI 3213231)

Rogers, C. R. (1946). *Significant aspects of client-centered therapy* [electronic version]. Retrieved March 30, 2009, from Web site: http://psychclassics.yorku.ca/Rogers/therapy.htm

Rovai, A. P. (2003). A practical framework for evaluating online distance education programs. *The Internet and Higher Education, 6,* 109-124.

Rovai, A. P. (2004). A constructivist approach to online college learning. *The Internet and Higher Education, 7*(2), 79-93.

Ruch, R. S. (2001). *Higher ed., inc.* Baltimore: The Johns Hopkins University Press.

Scott, J. C. (2005). The Chautauqua vision of liberal education. *History of Education, 34*(1), 41-59.

Senge, P. (1997). Communities of leaders and learners. *Harvard Business Review, 75*(5), 30–32.

Shale, D., & Gomes, J. (1998). Performance indicators and university distance education providers. *The Journal of Distance Education, 13*(1), 1-20.

Siemens, H. (2007). *Online education leadership practices of California community college administrators* (Dissertation, University of Virginia, UMI 3202502)

Sims, R. (1999). Interactivity on stage: Strategies for learner-designer communication. *Australian Journal of Education Technology, 15*(3), 257–272. Retreived April 30, 2009, from http://www.ascilite.org.au/ajet/ajet15/sims.html

Singh, G., O'Donoghue, J., & Betts, C. (2002). A UK study into the potential effects of virtual education: Does online learning spell an end for on-campus learning? *Behaviour & Information Technology*, 21(3), 223-229.

Singh, H. (2003). Building effective learning programs. *Educational Technology, 43*(6), 51-54.

Southern Association of Colleges and Schools. (2006). *Distance education policy*. Retrieved September 30, 2008, from http://www.sacscoc.org/pdf/081705/distance%20education.pdf

Stevenson, K. (2007). Motivating and inhibiting factors affecting faculty participation in online distance education *(Dissertation, East Carolina University, 2007)*. UMI 3285215.

Swanson, R. A., & Holton III, E. F. (2005). *Research in organizations: Foundations and methods of inquiry*. San Francisco: Berrett-Koehler.

Schaffhauser, D. (2009). *Survey reports many online learners never seek help before dropping out.*

Retrieved April 30, 2009, from Campus Technology Web site:
http://campustechnology.com/articles/2009/01/09/survey-reports-many-online-learners-never-seek-help-before-dropping-out.aspx

Su, B. (2006). Experiences of and preferences for interactive instructional activities in online learning environment. (*Dissertation, Indiana University, 2006*). UMI 3215221.

Tapscott, D., & Williams, A. D. (2008). *Wikinomics: How mass collaboration changes everything.* New York: Penguin Group.

Thill, J. V., & Bovee, C. L. (2007). *Excellence in Business Communication* (7th ed.). Upper Saddle River, NJ: Pearson Prentice Hall.

Thompson, A. A., Strickland, A. J., & Gamble, J. E. (2005). *Crafting and executing strategy.* New York: McGraw-Hill.

Tech & Learning. (2009, January). Mobile learning. Retrieved January 14, 2009, from http://www.nxtbook.com/nxtbooks/newbay/tl_200901/

Tough, A. (1982). *Intentional changes: A fresh approach to helping people change.* Chicago: Follett.

Traylor, S. (2009). The future is in your hand. *Tech & Learning, 29*(6), 27-30.

Turoff, M., Howard, C., & Discenza, R. (2005). *Technology's role in distance education.* In Encyclopedia of Information Science and Technology. Retrieved March 28, 2009, from Capella University Virtual Reference Library Web site: <http://find.galegroup.com.library.capella.edu/gvrl/infomark.do?&contentSet=EBKS&type=retrieve&tabID=T001&prodId=GVRL&docId=CX3466500539&eisbn=1-59140-794-X&source=gale&userGroupName=minn04804&version=1.0>.

Tyler-Smith, K. (2006). *Early attrition among first time elearners: A review of factors that contribute to drop-out, withdrawal and non-completion rates of adult learners undertaking elearning programmes.* Retrieved April 30, 2009, from MERLOT Journal of Online Learning and Teaching Web site: http://jolt.merlot.org/Vol2_No2_TylerSmith.htm

University of Phoenix. (2009). Online and campus programs. Retrieved April 25, 2009, from University of Phoenix Web site: http://www.phoenix.edu/online_and_campus_programs/degree_programs.html

Waits, T., & Lewis, L. (2003). Distance education at degree-granting postsecondary institutions: 2000-2001. *National Center for Education Statistics,* NCES 2003-17.

Webb, H. W., Gill, G., & Poe, G. (2005). Teaching with the case method online: Pure versus hybrid approaches. *Decision Sciences Journal of Innovative Education, (3)*2, 223-250.

Wickett, R. (2005). Adult learning theories and theological education. *Journal of Adult Theological Education, 2*(2), 53-161.

Yu, A. (1998). *An input-process-output structural framework for evaluating web-based instructions.* Retrieved March 23, 2009, from http://www.creative-wisdom.com/teaching/assessment/structural.html

Zhang, D. (2003). Powering e-learning in the new millennium: An overview of e-learning and enabling technology. *Information Systems Frontiers, 5*(2), 201-212.

Zhang, D., Zhao, J., Zhou, L., & Nunamaker, J. (2004). Can e-learning replace classroom learning? *Communications of the ACM, 47*(5), 75–79.

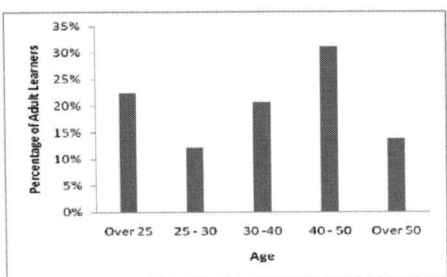

Figure A1. Percentage of Adult Learners by Age

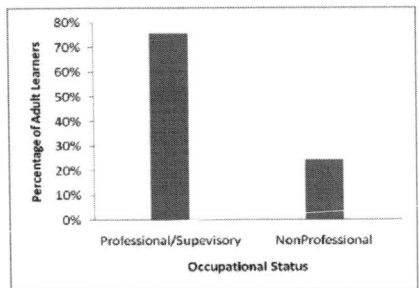

Figure A2. Percentage of Adult Learners by Occupational Status

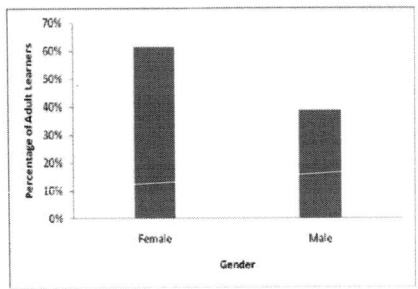

Figure A3. Percentage of Adult Learners by Gender

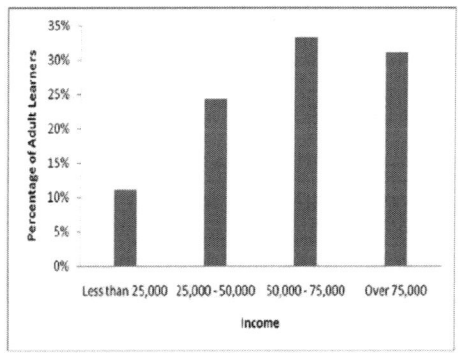

Figure A4. Percentage of Adult Learners by Income

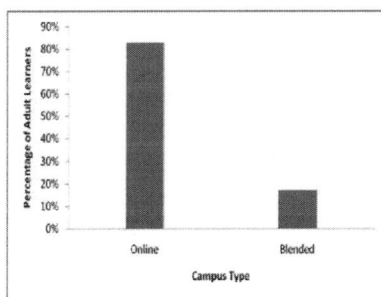

Figure A5. Percentage of Adult Learners by Campus Type

96

APPENDIX B. E-LEARNING MEDIA USE BY AGE CHI-SQUARE GOODNESS-OF-FIT TESTS

Table B1

E-Learning Media Use for Adult Learners over 25

Category	f	Total X^2
Announcements	13	0.38741
Syllabus	13	0.38741
Comments	13	0.38741
Live Web Conference	12	0.10247
Classroom Discussion Board	12	0.10247
Multimedia Text	12	0.10247
Multimedia Activity	12	0.10247
Course Materials	12	0.10247
Internet Articles	12	0.10247
Recorded Web Conferences	11	0.00032
Group Discussion Board	11	0.00032
Multimedia Presentation	11	0.00032
Multimedia Questions	11	0.00032
E-Mails	10	0.08096
Posting Files	10	0.08096
Instant Messages	8	0.79064
Text Messages	3	5.76376
Total X^2		8.49462

Note. $f_e = 10.9412$. $df = 16$. The critical value = 26.296. $\alpha = 0.05$. $p = 0.933$.

Table B2

E-Learning Media Use for Adult Learners 25 -30

Category	f	Total X^2
Live Web Conference	3	1.24081
Recorded Web Conferences	6	0.02206
Instant Messages	5	0.07414
E-Mails	7	0.32414
Classroom Discussion Board	7	0. 32414
Group Discussion Board	7	0. 32414
Text Messages	1	3.82414
Posting Files	6	0.02206
Multimedia Presentation	4	0.48039
Multimedia Text	7	0. 32414
Multimedia Questions	5	0.07414
Multimedia Activity	4	0.48039
Course Materials	6	0.02206
Announcements	7	0. 32414
Internet Articles	7	0. 32414
Syllabus	7	0. 32414
Comments	7	0 32414
Total X^2		8.83333

Note. f_e = 5.64706. *df* = 16. The critical value = 26.296. α = 0.05. *p* = 0.920.

Table B3

E-Learning Media Use for Adult Learners 30 – 40

Category	f	Total X^2
Announcements	12	0. 74917
Internet Articles	12	0. 74917
Classroom Discussion Board	11	0. 29005
Group Discussion Board	11	0. 29005
Live Web Conference	10	0.04477
Recorded Web Conferences	10	0.04477
E-Mails	10	0.04477
Posting Files	10	0.04477
Multimedia Text	10	0.04477
Multimedia Questions	10	0.04477
Multimedia Activity	10	0.04477
Course Materials	10	0.04477
Syllabus	10	0.04477
Comments	10	0.04477
Multimedia Presentation	9	0.01332
Instant Messages	3	4.31521
Text Messages	1	7.45986
Total X^2		14.3145

Note. f_e = 9.35294. df = 16. The critical value = 26.296. α = 0.05. p = 0.575.

Table B4

E-Learning Media Use for Adult Learners 40 – 50

Category	f	Total X^2
E-Mails	18	1.2213
Classroom Discussion Board	18	1.2213
Group Discussion Board	17	0. 7001
Announcements	17	0. 7001
Comments	17	0. 7001
Internet Articles	16	0. 3230
Recorded Web Conferences	15	0.0900
Posting Files	15	0.0900
Multimedia Text	15	0. 0900
Live Web Conference	14	0.0010
Multimedia Presentation	14	0.0010
Syllabus	14	0. 0010
Course Materials	13	0.0561
Multimedia Questions	12	0.2552
Instant Messages	11	0.5985
Multimedia Activity	9	1.7171
Text Messages	1	11.9544
Total X^2		19.7203

Note. f_e = 13.8824. *df* = 16. The critical value = 26.296. α = 0.05. *p* = 0.233.

Table B5

E-Learning Media Use for Adult Learners over 50

Category	f	Total X^2
Live Web Conference	8	0. 20284
E-Mails	8	0.20284
Classroom Discussion Board	8	0. 20284
Multimedia Text	8	0. 20284
Course Materials	8	0. 20284
Announcements	8	0. 20284
Internet Articles	8	0. 20284
Syllabus	8	0. 20284
Comments	8	0. 20284
Recorded Web Conferences	7	0.00456
Group Discussion Board	7	0. 00456
Multimedia Presentation	7	0. 00456
Multimedia Questions	7	0. 00456
Posting Files	6	0.09939
Multimedia Activity	6	0.09939
Instant Messages	3	2.14249
Text Messages	1	4.97008
Total X^2		9.15517

Note. f_e = 6.82353. df = 16. The critical value = 26.296. α = 0.05. p = 0.907.

Table C1
E-Learning Media Use Comparison by Age

Age Group	Live Web Conference	Recorded Web Conference	Instant Messaging	E-mails	Classroom DB	Group DB	Text Messages	Postings Assignments	Comments
				E-Learning Media					
Over 25									
f	12.000	11.000	8.000	10.000	12.000	11.000	3.000	10.000	13.000
f_e	11.020	11.490	7.040	12.430	13.130	12.430	1.640	11.020	12.900
X^2	0.086	0.021	0.132	0.476	0.098	0.165	1.123	0.095	0.001
25-30									
f	3.000	6.000	5.000	7.000	7.000	7.000	1.000	6.000	7.000
f_e	5.690	5.930	3.630	6.420	6.780	6.420	0.850	5.690	6.660
X^2	1.272	0.001	0.515	0.053	0.001	0.053	0.027	0.017	0.018
30 - 40									
f	10.000	10.000	3.000	10.000	11.000	11.000	1.000	10.000	10.000
f_e	9.420	9.820	6.020	10.630	11.230	10.630	1.400	9.420	11.030
X^2	0.035	0.003	1.511	0.037	0.001	0.013	0.116	0.035	0.096
40 - 50									
f	14.000	15.000	11.000	18.000	18.000	17.000	1.000	15.000	17.000
f_e	13.990	14.580	8.930	15.770	16.670	15.770	2.080	13.990	16.370
X^2	0.000	0.012	0.481	0.314	0.107	0.095	0.563	0.073	0.024
Over 50									
f	8.000	7.000	3.000	8.000	8.000	7.000	1.000	6.000	8.000
f_e	6.880	7.170	4.390	7.750	8.190	7.750	1.020	6.880	8.050
X^2	0.184	0.004	0.439	0.001	0.004	0.073	0.001	0.111	0.000

Table C1 (continued)
E-Learning Media Comparison Use by Age

Age Group	Multimedia Presentation	Multimedia Text	Multimedia Questions	E-Learning Media Multimedia Activity	Course Material	Announcements	Internet Articles	Syllabus
Over 25								
f	11.000	12.000	11.000	12.000	12.000	13.000	12.000	13.000
f_e	10.550	12.200	10.560	9.620	11.490	13.370	12.900	12.200
X^2	0.019	0.003	0.019	0.591	0.022	0.100	0.063	0.053
25 -30								
f	4.000	7.000	5.000	4.000	6.000	7.000	7.000	7.000
f_e	5.450	6.300	5.450	4.960	5.930	6.900	6.660	6.300
X^2	0.385	0.079	0.037	0.187	0.001	0.001	0.018	0.079
30 - 40								
f	9.000	10.000	10.000	10.000	10.000	12.000	12.000	10.000
f_e	9.020	10.430	9.020	8.220	9.820	11.490	11.030	10.430
X^2	0.000	0.017	0.106	0.385	0.003	0.029	0.086	0.017
40 - 50								
f	14.000	15.000	12.000	9.000	13.000	17.000	16.000	14.000
f_e	13.390	15.480	13.390	12.200	14.580	16.960	16.370	15.480
X^2	0.028	0.015	0.145	0.540	0.172	0.000	0.008	0.141
Over 50								
f	7.000	8.000	7.000	6.000	8.000	8.000	8.000	8.000
f_e	6.580	7.610	6.580	6.000	7.170	8.340	8.050	7.610
X^2	0.026	0.020	0.026	0.000	0.097	0.014	0.000	0.020

Note. DB = Discussion Board. One cell with an expected count less than one. Five cells with expected counts less than five. $df = 64$. Critical value $= 83.675$. $\alpha = 0.05$. $X^2 = 12.268$. Chi-square approximation probably invalid.

Table C2

E-Learning Media Use Comparison by Age without Text Messaging

Age Group	Live Web Conference	Recorded Web Conference	Instant Messaging	E-mails	Classroom DB	Group DB	Postings Assignments	Comments
Over 25								
f	12.000	11.000	8.000	10.000	12.000	11.000	10.000	13.000
f_e	10.920	11.410	6.980	12.340	13.040	12.340	10.940	12.810
X^2	0.102	0.015	0.148	0.444	0.083	0.145	0.081	0.003
25 -30								
f	3.000	6.000	5.000	7.000	7.000	7.000	6.000	7.000
f_e	5.680	5.920	3.630	6.4.0	6.770	6.410	5.680	6.650
X^2	1.265	0.001	0.521	0.055	0.0008	0.055	0.018	0.019
30 - 40								
f	10.000	10.000	3.000	10.000	11.000	11.000	10.000	10.000
f_e	9.450	9.850	6.030	10.650	11.260	10.650	9.450	11.060
X^2	0.032	0.002	1.523	0.040	0.006	0.011	0.032	0.101
40 - 50								
f	14.000	15.000	11.000	18.000	18.000	17.000	15.000	17.000
f_e	14.050	14.580	8.970	15.850	16.740	15.770	14.050	16.440
X^2	0.000	0.008	0.460	0.293	0.094	0.084	0.064	0.019
Over 50								
f	8.000	7.000	3.000	3.000	8.000	7.000	6.000	8.000
f_e	6.880	7.170	4.390	7.750	8.190	7.750	6.880	8.050
X^2	0.184	0.004	0.440	0.0008	0.005	0.073	0.112	0.000

Table C2 (continued)
E-Learning Media Use by Age without Text Messaging

Age Group	Multimedia Presentation	Multimedia Text	Multimedia Questions	E-Learning Media Multimedia Activity	Course Material	Announcements	Internet Articles	Syllabus
Over 25								
f	11.000	12.000	11.000	12.000	12.000	13.000	12.000	13.000
f_e	10.480	12.110	10.480	9.550	11.410	13.270	12.810	12.110
X^2	0.026	0.001	0.026	0.631	0.031	0.006	0.051	0.066
25 -30								
f	4.000	7.000	5.000	4.000	6.000	7.000	7.000	7.000
f_e	5.450	6.300	5.440	4.960	5.920	6.890	6.650	6.280
X^2	0.381	0.081	0.035	0.184	0.001	0.002	0.019	0.081
30 - 40								
f	9.000	10.000	10.000	10.000	10.000	12.000	12.000	10.000
f_e	9.050	10.450	9.050	8.240	9.850	11.460	11.060	10.450
X^2	0.000	0.020	0.101	0.375	0.002	0.026	0.081	0.020
40 - 50								
f	14.000	15.000	12.000	9.000	13.000	17.000	16.000	14.000
f_e	13.450	15.550	13.450	12.260	14.650	17.040	16.440	15.550
X^2	0.022	0.019	0.157	0.866	0.186	0.000	0.012	0.154
Over 50								
f	7.000	8.000	7.000	6.000	8.000	8.000	8.000	8.000
f_e	6.580	7.610	6.580	6.000	7.170	8.340	8.050	7.610
X^2	0.026	0.020	0.026	0.000	0.097	0.014	0.000	0.020

Note. DB = Discussion Board. df = 60. Critical value = 79.082. α = 0.05. X^2 =10.422. p = 1.000.